MAKING A
STRONG CHRISTIAN NATION

HOW TO LIVE GOD'S PLAN FOR THE USA

Steven Andrew

Pastor - USA Christian Ministries
www.USAChristianMinistries.com

ACTS ONE EIGHT Publishing

MAKING A
STRONG CHRISTIAN NATION

HOW TO LIVE GOD'S PLAN FOR THE USA

ISBN 9780977955077
Copyright © 2011 by Steven Andrew

Published by ACTS ONE EIGHT Publishing
ActsOneEightPublishing.com

Table of Contents

BY THE PRESIDENT OF THE
UNITED STATES OF AMERICA: A PROCLAMATION.

WHEREAS, the Senate of the United States, devoutly recognizing the Supreme Authority and just Government of Almighty God, in all the affairs of men and of nations...

And whereas it is the duty of nations as well as of men, to own their dependence upon the overruling power of God, to confess their sins and transgressions, in humble sorrow, yet with assured hope that genuine repentance will lead to mercy and pardon; and to recognize the sublime truth, announced in the Holy Scriptures and proven by all history, that those nations only are blessed whose God is the Lord: And, insomuch as we know that, by His divine law, nations, like individuals, are subjected to punishments and chastisements in this world...

We have grown in numbers, wealth, and power as no other nation has ever grown. But we have forgotten God. We have forgotten the gracious hand which preserved us in peace, and multiplied and enriched and strengthened us; and we have vainly imagined, in the deceitfulness of our hearts, that all these blessings were produced by some superior wisdom and virtue of our own. Intoxicated with unbroken success, we have become too self-sufficient to feel the necessity of redeeming and preserving grace, too proud to pray to the God that made us!

It behooves us, then, to humble ourselves before the offended Power, to confess our national sins, and to pray for clemency and forgiveness...

ॐ∞

But for [the Bible], we would not know right from wrong.

Abraham Lincoln

Preface

Are you ready to make a strong Christian nation?

Since 2008 I have prayed a powerful, yet simple, prayer that has enhanced my relationship with God and my knowledge of our Christian nation. The prayer is: "Father, what are Your best plans for the USA? In Jesus' name. Amen."

Will you agree that God's loving answer to this prayer is to have mercy for the USA and to unite the USA in Christ? I invite you now to learn the Biblical revelation that God has shared with me on how to unite our Christian nation and answer God's call for us. As Christians we know that "with God all things are possible." I trust that you will be inspired to join together with Christians across our nation—so that we can see God's best plans come about. As God's USA family let's thank God for His love, faithfulness and miraculous help that He gives to us. Also, as you read this book, I invite you to ask God to show you how you can get involved in *Making a Strong Christian Nation*.

God loves you.

Pastor Steven Andrew, USA Christian Ministries
Psalm 33:12

ହ∼ର

I thank God for each person who reviewed the manuscript. Your suggestions have made this a better book. I appreciate you; God delights in you. May God strengthen you in Jesus' name!

1

The USA Needs God

Father,

What are Your best plans for the USA?

Show me what I can do to strengthen our

Christian nation.

In Jesus' name. Amen.

W ould you like to know what God's best plans are for the USA? Do you also desire for our nation to walk remarkably close with God and to be filled with the hope and blessings of Jesus Christ? Starting with our Founding Fathers, Americans have lived for God, spread Christianity boldly and worked diligently for Him. In Christ we have gained God's favor for our nation. Whenever we turn to God, we find His answers. Let's now look at how our first permanent settlers faithfully established our nation's foundation on Jesus Christ–in an everlasting covenant.

Beginning in 1607, we discover the Jamestown Settlers coming ashore. What was their priority on arriving? The

Jamestown settlers' *first acts* were to pray, fast, place a large cross on the Virginia beach and *covenant* America to God. Our nation's Christian covenant dedication says:

> **We do hereby dedicate this Land, and ourselves, to reach the People within these shores with the Gospel of Jesus Christ, and to raise up Godly generations after us, and with these generations take the Kingdom of God to all the earth. <u>May this Covenant of Dedication remain to all generations,</u> as long as this earth remains, and may this Land, along with England, be [an] Evangelist to the World. May all who see this Cross, remember what we have done here, and may those who come here to inhabit join us in this Covenant and in this most noble work that the Holy Scriptures may be fulfilled.**

When our Christian Founding Fathers crossed the ocean to settle, they saw it as an opportunity to raise up a Christian nation that included God in every area. They made covenant with God and authored Christian documents that would govern a people under God. They set aside days of prayer and fasting as well as thanksgiving. The Pilgrims, George Washington, John Adams and our Founding Fathers remained in covenant with the LORD. Following the one true God for hundreds of years has brought unprecedented prosperity and life to the USA. God made us the greatest nation in the world. This is because Americans have seen fulfilled God's wonderful promise in Psalm 33:12:

> **Blessed is the nation whose God is the LORD, the people He has chosen as His own inheritance.**

As a result of Jesus' love flowing through us, we are the most benevolent people in all of history. Fulfilling the Jamestown settler's prophetic declaration, Americans have sacrificially released the greatest missionary force ever. We have brought the good news of Jesus Christ to the world. Our missionaries have founded schools, orphanages, churches and hospitals in the USA and across the world. When a nation needs help, we respond as Good Samaritans. Our Christian morals of God's mercy, integrity and freedom are a light to the world. We have wealth beyond all other nations. No nation has seen their Constitution last for more than 200 years, except the USA. Go just about anywhere in the world

Congress Seeking God: George Washington (center in black coat), John Adams (sixth from top left), Samuel Adams (light coat to left of John Adams), Benjamin Franklin (second from top right) and Patrick Henry (first on left kneeling)

9

and you are received and respected. And when you come home you realize, nobody has it as good as we do. God has indeed blessed the USA!

However, we find that in recent years Satan, through deception and a small minority, has been trying to lead the USA astray from our nation's foundation on Christ. Decisions have been made opposing God and our Founding Fathers, including against the Christian laws they made for us. This ungodly minority deceptively says they respect George Washington, Abraham Lincoln and often God, but then they act and make laws against them. As a result of disobeying God, the USA has seen trouble after trouble. Anytime the economy recedes, the military declines or fewer children are raised by both their father and mother, then we should ask: Why are we missing God's blessing?

God says that sin is the reason we miss His blessings. It is why His protection can be removed. National sins affect all of us with great trouble. After having unsurpassed wealth, the USA became the largest debtor nation in history. As a result of the government debt, Americans lose their personal money in more taxes. The Holy Bible describes this as plundering. This means children have less, families argue over finances and business owners offer fewer jobs. Corruption and betrayal have spread to parts of the government. 71% have been angry with the Federal government (Rasmussen Reports, 2010). National security has decreased. Endless and winless wars have been fought. The government has refused to protect our borders and has given many foreigners better treatment than our citizens. Morals, relationships and brotherly love also declined. Some schools have forbidden the American flag and politicians have focused on things that both God and our Founding Fathers' laws forbid, including abortions, not

10

honoring the elderly and promoting sexual sin. It is the wrong direction. With so much trouble, we must wonder why does this happen?

God Lets Nations Choose Him or Reject Him

Searching God's Word, we find God's desire to dwell with His people, including our Christian nation (Psalm 33:12, Matthew 28:19-20). However, God allows each nation to choose Him, or not. We choose between life and good, or death and evil. This Biblical principle also applies to the USA. We find this key in Deuteronomy 30:15-18. It reads:

> **See, I have set before you today life and good, death and evil, in that I command you today to love the LORD your God, to walk in His ways, and to keep His commandments, His statutes, and His judgments, that you may live and multiply; and the LORD your God will bless you in the land which you go to possess.**
>
> **But if your heart turns away so that you do not hear, and are drawn away, and worship other gods and serve them, I announce to you today that you shall surely perish; you shall not prolong your days in the land which you cross over... to go in and possess.**

Our nation needs God. Jesus is the answer for the USA. He is the only one who gives hope, love and protection to us. Look to Jesus. He reaches out His hands to every American to come to Him. God has a plan of prosperity and life for us, not disaster and death. By living for God, we find our greatest purpose. Isaiah 42:6 shows that God created us and why following God matters. The Holy Bible says:

11

> **God, the LORD, created the heavens and stretched them out. He created the earth and everything in it. He gives breath and life to everyone in all the world.**

Do you see that Jesus gives life? In John 10:10, He says:

> **I have come that they may have life, and that they may have it more abundantly.**

Our Declaration of Independence uses these Biblical truths to cite King George III's disobedience to God. Using God's Word, our Founding Fathers had God's authority for independence. To gain Christian freedom, they declared:

> **...all men are created equal that they are endowed by their Creator with certain unalienable rights, that among these are life, liberty, and the pursuit of happiness.**

Two Questions that God Wants to Answer

God is the source of life, liberty and happiness. Turning to God is always the answer for the USA. He promises to forgive our sins and heal our land as we do (2 Chronicles 7:14). God calls the USA to seek Him. Jesus says, "Ask, and it will be given to you; seek, and you will find; knock, and it will be opened to you" (Matthew 7:7). To understand how we are to live for God, will you ask Him:

1) What are Your best plans for the USA? (Matthew 7:7)

2) What does the Holy Bible say that I can do to strengthen our Christian nation? (2 Timothy 3:16-17)

As you pray this, listen to God for His answers.

12

2

The Settlers, Pilgrims, Washington, Adams…
Made the USA a Christian Nation Forever

Father,

We thank You and praise You that we are a

Christian nation from our beginning and forever.

In Jesus' name. Amen.

D o you see that our Founding Fathers dedicated our nation to God for the advancement of the Christian faith and for God's glory? Some ungodly people have tried to censor and lie about our Founding Fathers who brought God into every aspect of American life. But God wants us to share these powerful Christian truths. If we today follow what our Founding Fathers did to obey God, then we will have the same results they did. Our Founding Fathers meant for every American to faithfully follow God.

The USA is a Covenant Christian Nation

From the Jamestown settlers' 1607 covenant dedication, to today, the USA has welcomed the LORD and His blessings. The Pilgrims signed the Mayflower Compact in 1620 that says, "Having undertaken for the Glory of God". Today, we affectionately sing, "God shed His grace on thee" in *America the Beautiful* and "God bless America".

13

What did our presidents testify about God? George Washington, who saw God miraculously favor him and the less powerful American revolutionary army, said:

> **...it is the duty of all Nations to acknowledge the providence of Almighty God, to obey his will, to be grateful for his benefits, and humbly to implore his protection and favor.** [1]

> **...To the distinguished character of patriot, it should be our highest glory to add the more distinguished character of Christian.** [1]

John Adams shared his allegiance to God by affirming:

> **The Christian religion is, above all the religions...** [1]

Similarly, Thomas Jefferson declared:

> **The Christian religion is the best religion that has ever been given to man...** [1]

Shouldn't we also say Christianity is above all religions today? As the intent of our Founding Fathers, we are to include God in Congress, our courts, schools and all government. Isn't it wrong not to include Almighty God? In the Gettysburg Address, Abraham Lincoln said:

> **...this nation under God...** [1]

And the Supreme Court declared:

> **...this is a Christian nation.** [1]

Our Christian nation's national motto is: "In God we trust". It is written on the Washington Monument, above where the Speaker of the House of Representatives sits, above the Senate door, and on our currency. We proudly sing, "And this be our motto: In God is our trust" in our Christian national anthem. Our Founding Fathers established for *only Christian prayer* to open government sessions. In 1777 Congress declared a day of thanksgiving and praise with:

> **...that it may please GOD, <u>through the Merits of Jesus Christ</u>... to afford his Blessing on the Governments of these States... to prosper the Means of [Christian] Religion for the promotion and enlargement of that Kingdom [of God] which consisteth "in Righteousness, Peace and Joy in the Holy Ghost."**

The House Judiciary Committee affirmed our Christian nation to have Christian chaplains by saying:

> **Resolved, that the daily sessions of this body be opened with prayer and that... <u>the [Christian] ministers of the Gospel</u>... are hereby requested to attend and alternately perform this solemn duty.**

There are crosses on our hills and on military graves of our soldiers around the world. All these crosses testify of our Christian nation. Since the USA is in covenant with God, He says that our nation belongs to Him. The USA is God's country. Now, let's go to the beginning, with the first settlers and see more details of our extraordinary faith and history.

Jamestown Settlers' Faith

America's founding shows that following Jesus Christ is what it means to be an American. *Our identity is in Christ.* When the Jamestown settlers arrived at Camp Henry (Virginia Beach), and planted a wood cross on the beach, they testified this land belongs to Jesus Christ. Rev. Robert Hunt, who was known as "honest, religious, courageous..." by Captain John Smith[2], led our first covenant prayer. As we saw, it includes:

15

> **May all who see this Cross [on America],
> remember what we have done here, and may those
> who come here to inhabit join us in this Covenant
> and in this most noble work that the Holy
> Scriptures may be fulfilled.**

Today, Christians across the USA are in agreement with the Jamestown Settlers planting the Cross that testifies that the LORD is our God. Do you see how we are to live for God and raise up godly generations? This prophetic prayer is being fulfilled. Looking at the Virginia Charter, we find the primary purpose, among others for the Jamestown Settlers, was to propagate the Christian religion. The charter reads:

> **We... by the Providence of Almighty God,
> hereafter tend to the Glory of his Divine Majesty,
> in propagating of Christian Religion to such
> People, as yet live in Darkness and miserable
> Ignorance of the true Knowledge and Worship of
> God...[3]**

Do you see their concern for the non-Christians who live in "darkness and miserable ignorance..." of God? "There is one God and one Mediator between God and men, the Man Christ Jesus" (1 Timothy 2:5). Jesus came for everyone. Upon arriving at Jamestown, Reverend Hunt gathered the men and prayed from Habakkuk 2:20: "The Lord is in His holy temple. Let all the earth keep silent before Him." As one of the first priorities, they built a church. Hunt led the people in prayer morning and evening. Here is a sample prayer:

> **Almighty God, ... we beseech Thee to bless us
> and this plantation which we and our nation have
> begun in Thy fear and for Thy glory... and seeing,
> Lord, the highest end of our plantation here is to
> set up the standard and display the banner of Jesus**

Christ, even here where Satan's throne is, Lord, let our labour be blessed in labouring for the conversion of the heathen... Lord, sanctify our spirits and give us holy hearts, that so we may be Thy instruments in this most glorious work.[3]

Pilgrims', Puritans'... Faith

When the Pilgrims arrived in 1620, we find their *Christian purpose in the Mayflower Compact,* which declares:

In the name of God, amen... Having undertaken for the glory of God, and advancement of the Christian faith... anno Domini, 1620

"Anno Domini" means "in the year of our Lord" Jesus Christ. Starting in 1630, the Puritans came to Massachusetts for Christian purposes. Puritan leader John Winthrop wrote:

We are <u>entered into covenant with Him</u> for this work. We have taken out a commission... but if we neglect to observe those articles, and... shall embrace this present world and prosecute [follow] our carnal intentions, seeking great things for ourselves and our prosperity, then the Lord will surely break out in wrath against us, and perjured be revenged of a perjured people, and He will make us know the price of the breach of such a covenant.

The Holy Bible: The First Textbook

It is easy to notice that the Pilgrims, Puritans and other settlers emphasized teaching all American children Christian faith from God's Word. The Holy Bible was the first text book in American schools and the foundation of education and American life. Our Founding Fathers were all taught the Bible and Christian prayer. The first American university, Harvard, which is named after a Puritan clergyman, required students "to know God and Jesus Christ". Harvard's motto was *Veritas Christo et Ecclesiae*, which means "Truth For Christ and the Church". The original student handbook directly says:

> **Let every student be plainly instructed and earnestly pressed to consider well: the main end of his life and studies is "to know God and Jesus Christ, which is eternal life" (John 17.3), and therefore to lay Christ in the bottom, as the only foundation of all sound knowledge and learning. And seeing the Lord only giveth wisdom, let everyone seriously set himself by prayer in secret to seek it of Him (Prov. 2.3).**

Laws to Fast for Sin and to Teach Children the Holy Bible

Our government made laws for fasting and prayer. For example, in Virginia it was mandatory for everyone to pray and fast for forgiveness and repentance of sins to avoid God's judgment. Virginia law declared:

> **WHEREAS the many sins of this country may justly provoke the anger of Almighty God against us, and draw down his judgments upon us, unless diverted by a timely and hearty repentance, the governor, council and burgesses of this grand assembly taking the same into their serious consideration, have enacted and do by these presents enact that the 27th day of August [1668] next be set apart for a day of humiliation, hereby strictly requiring all persons on that day to repair [go to] to their respective parish churches, with**

18

fasting and prayers to implore God's mercy and deprecate the evils justly impending over us; And be it further enacted that if any person or persons in contempt hereof shall be found on that day working, gaming, or drinking (works of necessity only excepted) he or they... shall be fined...[4]

American laws required every child to be taught Christianity. For example, *"The Book of The General Laws 1685"* in Plymouth required parents to teach their children how to live as a Christian, to know salvation in Christ and how to read the Holy Bible.[5] Knowing God is the highest priority for children. Do you see why the Holy Bible and Christian prayer are so important to have back in school?

God's Laws Are Our Laws

Studying our laws, we find that our Founding Fathers made God's laws our laws. The Holy Bible is the foundation of our laws. The first written code of laws in America is founded from the Ten Commandments. Let's look at examples of the first and third commandments in the 1610 Virginia colony law:

Law Referencing the First Commandment

[S]ince we owe our highest and supreme duty, our greatest and all our allegiance to Him from whom all power and authority is derived, and flows as from the first and only fountain, and being especially soldiers impressed in this sacred cause, we must alone expect our success from Him who is only the blesser of all good attempts, the King of kings, the Commander of commanders, and Lord of hosts, I do strictly command and charge all Captains and Officers of what quality or nature soever... to have a care that the Almighty God be

19

**duly and daily served, and that they call upon their
people to hear sermons, as that also they diligently
frequent morning and evening prayer themselves
by their own example and daily life and duties
herein, encouraging others thereunto.**

Law Referencing the Third Commandment
**That no man speak impiously or maliciously
against the holy and blessed Trinity or any of the
three persons...**

All of the Ten Commandments are found as laws in our
American history. For example, the Supreme Court endorsed
an 1824 Supreme Court of Pennsylvania case that noted:

**The late Judge Wilson, of the [original]
Supreme Court of the United States... had just
risen from his seat in the Convention which formed
the Constitution of the United States, and of this
State; and it is well known that for our present
form of government we are greatly indebted to his
exertions and influence. With his fresh recollection
of both constitutions, in his course of Lectures (3d
vol. of his works, 112), he states that profaneness
and blasphemy [of God as written in the Ten
Commandments] are offences punishable by fine
and imprisonment, and that <u>Christianity is part of
the common law.</u>**

The Declaration of Independence Endorses and Relies on God

Shouldn't every student today know our nation's covenant
to follow God? The signers of the Declaration of
Independence said they "mutually pledge to each other our
lives, our fortunes, and our sacred honor" to establish the

The Signers of the Declaration of Independence
(John Adams center in white pants, John Hancock sitting on right)

USA with Christian freedom. Have you realized that freedom only comes from God? Be careful of anyone who wants freedom but without God. Our Declaration of Independence endorses God in government and acknowledges that *we are created by God* with liberty. Our Founding Fathers declared:

> **...to which the laws of nature and of nature's God entitles them... We hold these truths to be self-evident, that all men are created equal, that they are endowed by their Creator with certain unalienable rights, that among these are life, liberty, and the pursuit of happiness. We, therefore, the Representatives of the United States of America, in general Congress assembled, appealing to the Supreme Judge of the world... for the support of this Declaration, with a firm reliance on the protection of Divine Providence...**

The Christian Faith of the Signers of the Declaration of Independence

The Holy Bible is the most quoted reference among our Founding Fathers. Talking about our Christian government, President John Quincy Adams said:

The Declaration of Independence laid the cornerstone of human government upon the first precepts of Christianity.

Let's now look at these quotes that the signers of the Declaration of Independence made. John Hancock is the famous big first signature on the Declaration.

John Hancock
...that all may bow to the Scepter of our LORD JESUS CHRIST, and the whole Earth be filled with his Glory. *As Governor to the People of Massachusetts*

John Adams
[The Fourth of July] ought to be commemorated as the day of deliverance by solemn acts of devotion to God Almighty.

Richard Stockton
...the fear of God is the beginning of wisdom...

John Witherspoon
Whoever is an avowed enemy of God, I scruple not to call him an enemy to his country.

Samuel Adams
I... [rely] upon the merits of Jesus Christ for a pardon of all my sins.

Thomas Jefferson

God who gave us life gave us liberty. Can the liberties of a nation be secure when we have removed a conviction that these liberties are the gift of God?

Charles Carroll

Grateful to Almighty God for the blessings which, through Jesus Christ Our Lord, He had conferred on my beloved country in her emancipation and on myself in permitting me, under circumstances of mercy... to survive the fiftieth year of independence, adopted by Congress on the 4th of July 1776...

Samuel Huntington

...that we may obtain forgiveness through the merits and mediation of our Lord and Savior Jesus Christ.

The Christian Faith of George Washington

Our most famous American, George Washington, is known as a humble man of prayer and a man of godly standards. He had prayer and Bible study in the morning and evening, as his nephew who lived with him witnessed.[6] Obeying God's Word, George Washington assured chiefs of the Delaware Indian tribe who brought their children to be trained in American (Christian) public schools the following:

I am glad you have brought three of the children of your principal chiefs to be educated with us... You do well to wish <u>to learn</u> our arts and ways of life, and <u>above all, the religion of Jesus</u>

23

<u>Christ.</u> These will make you a greater and happier people than you are. <u>Congress will do everything they can to assist you in this wise intention...</u>

Notice George Washington says, "to learn... above all, the religion of Jesus Christ. These will make you a greater and happier people than you are." And that "Congress will do everything they can to assist you in this wise intention". Also, do you remember Washington kneeling in earnest prayer at Valley Forge and elsewhere to seek God's help to win the battles? This USA stamp documents this. Only by trusting in God could we conquer the greatest military of the time.

George Washington Praying at Valley Forge

Look again at what George Washington teaches regarding governing. He tells Americans:

> **By the President of the United States of America... it is the duty of all nations to acknowledge the providence of Almighty God, to obey His will...**

The use of the word "nations" means that George Washington's actions and intent are for God to be in government. Washington humbly also knew he wasn't perfect as only Jesus is without sin. That is why he asked God to forgive him. Here is a prayer of forgiveness of sins, trusting in Jesus' blood for atonement, from Washington's prayer book:

> **Oh, eternal and everlasting God, direct my thoughts, words and work. Wash away my sins in the immaculate blood of the Lamb and purge my heart by Thy Holy Spirit. Daily, frame me more and more in the likeness of Thy son, Jesus Christ, that living in Thy fear, and dying in Thy favor, I may in thy appointed time obtain the resurrection of the justified unto eternal life.**

The Faith of John Adams

John Adams was our first Vice-president and second President. As a bold Christian, he was involved in the Continental Congress and a signer of the Declaration of Independence, the Bill of Rights and more. In signing the Treaty of Paris in 1783, for the independence of the American states, John Adams, John Jay and Benjamin Franklin signed the treaty which started and ended with:

> **In the name of the most holy and undivided Trinity... in the year of our Lord, one thousand seven hundred and eighty-three.**

25

As a godly man, John Adams only approved of a Christian government. He said:

> There is no authority, civil or religious—there can be no legitimate government but what is administered by this Holy Ghost. There can be no salvation without it. All without it is rebellion and perdition, or in more orthodox words, damnation.

Like George Washington, John Adams called the USA to prayer, fasting and repentance. Our USA government declared:

> I [John Adams] hereby recommend accordingly, that Thursday, the twenty-fifth of April next, be observed throughout the United States of America as a day of solemn humiliation, fasting, and prayer; that the citizens on that day abstain, as far as may be, from their secular occupation, and devote the time to the sacred duties of [Christian] religion, in public and in private; that they call to mind our numerous offenses against the most high God, confess them before Him with the sincerest penitence, implore His pardoning mercy, through the Great Mediator and Redeemer [Jesus Christ], for our past transgressions, and that through His Holy Spirit, we may be disposed and enabled to yield a more suitable obedience to His righteous requisitions in time to come; that He would interpose to arrest the progress of that impiety and licentiousness in principle and practice so offensive to Himself and so ruinous to mankind; that He would make us deeply sensible that "righteousness exalteth a nation, but sin is a reproach to any people" [Proverbs 14:34].

The USA Government is Founded on God and the Holy Bible

Do you know which Bible verse gave our Founding Fathers direction to build a government that included God in all parts of it? They searched and found the three branches of government, of which God is in, with Isaiah 33:22. This Scripture says:

For the LORD is our Judge, the LORD is our Lawgiver, the LORD is our King; He will save us;

First Act of Congress: Pray and Read the Bible

Our Founding Fathers' intent is for God to be part of all American government. For example, *the first act of Congress* was to have a Christian minister open Congress by a prayer ending in Jesus' name in 1774. Congress also read the Holy Bible, including Psalm 35. John Adams noted how meaningful the Scripture was. Furthering this intent, Congress, as well as George Washington, authorized the government to pay Christian chaplains for Congress and the military.

Government Taught Christianity in Schools

Benjamin Franklin instructed public school children about the supremacy of Jesus Christ. Pennsylvania schools taught:

…the excellency of the Christian religion above all others, ancient or modern.

The popular New England Primer was based on the Holy Bible, as the McGuffey reader was afterward. Look at the New England Primer school alphabet lesson using Bible verses:

27

Biblical Alphabet School Lesson for American Children

A WISE son makes a glad father, but a foolish son is the heaviness of his mother.

BETTER is a little, with the fear of the Lord, than great treasure, and trouble therewith.

COME unto Christ, all ye who labor and are heavy hiden, and he will give you rest.

DO NOT the abominable thing which I hate, saith the Lord.

EXCEPT a man be born again, he cannot see the kingdom of God.

FOOLISHNESS is bound up in the heart of a child, but the rod of correction will drive it from him.

GRIEVE not the Holy Spirit, lest it depart from thee.

HOLINESS becomes God's house for ever.

IT is good for me to draw near unto God.

KEEP thy heart with all diligence, for out of it are the issues of life.

LIARS will have their part in the lake which burns with fire and brimstone.

MANY are the afflictions of the righteous but the Lord delivers them out of them all.

NOW is the accepted time; now is the day of salvation.

OUT of the abundance of the heart thy mouth speaketh.

PRAY to thy Father who is in secret, and, thy Father who sees in secret will reward thee openly.

QUIT you like men; be strong; stand fast in the faith.

REMEMBER thy Creator in the days of thy youth.

28

SALVATION belongeth unto the Lord.

TRUST in God at all times, ye people; pour out your hearts before him.

UPON the wicked God will rain a horrible tempest.

WOE to the wicked; it will be ill with him, for the reward of his hand will be given him.

EXHORT one another daily while it is called today, lest any of you be hardened through the deceitfulness of sin.

YOUNG men, you have overcome the wicked one.

ZEAL hath consumed me, because my enemies have forgotten the word of God.

Congress not only read but also recommended the Holy Bible. For example, when a recommendation for "a neat edition of the Holy Scriptures for the use of schools" came to Congress, the 1782 government approval was:

...the United States in Congress assembled... recommend this edition of the Bible to the inhabitants of the United States.[8]

Our Founding Fathers Held Ongoing Christian Church Meetings in the USA Capital

In 1800 Congress authorized Christian church services in the USA Capital. By 1865, the Capital Christian church contained the "largest Protestant Sabbath audience,"[7] the largest church.

Christian Laws for Everyone

With love for God our Founding Fathers required everyone to follow our nation's Christian laws, including non-

29

Christians. If someone did not want to follow our nation's laws, then they were not welcome and/or jailed. In the first extensive commentary on our Constitution, *Supreme Court Justice Joseph Story explained that the First Amendment means Christianity only, not any other belief.* This is the intent of our Founding Fathers. Justice Story's popular 1833 work was reprinted for 72 years. He had been on the Supreme Court since 1811 and he wrote:

> **The real object of the [First] Amendment was, not to countenance [approve], much less to advance Mohammedanism, or Judaism, or infidelity [secularism], by prostrating Christianity, but to exclude all rivalry among Christian sects [denominations]...**

The First Amendment of our Christian nation says:

> **Congress shall make no law respecting an establishment of [one Christian denomination] religion, or prohibiting the free exercise [of Christian religion] thereof...**

The First Amendment is not meant for other religions but to allow Americans to practice Christianity in their Christian denomination. Our Founding Fathers declared independence with God's liberty. Also notice the oaths taken in our nation to God on the Holy Bible. By including the Holy Bible we show this is to the LORD not a foreign god. It is important to understand these two points about our Founding Fathers. They believed:

1. Christian faith is the most important part of life, and

2. USA freedom is for Christian freedom, not all "freedoms".

30

All 50 States Endorse God

Are you aware that every state's Constitution acknowledges and worships God? Examples are:

Pennsylvania, 1776–Preamble
"We, the people... grateful to Almighty God for the blessings of civil and [Christian] religious liberty, and humbly invoking His guidance..."

Texas, 1845–Preamble
"Humbly invoking the blessings of Almighty God, the People of the State of Texas do ordain and establish this Constitution."

Alabama, 1901–Preamble
"We the people of the State of Alabama, invoking the favor and guidance of Almighty God, do ordain and establish the following Constitution..."

The USA is Founded on Jesus Christ

Have you thought who started our Christian laws for our nation? Our Founding Fathers did. Here George Washington orders the military to attend church and to act like a Christian:

The commander-in-chief directs that divine service be performed every Sunday at eleven o'clock in those brigades which there are chaplains; those which have none [are] to attend the places of worship nearest to them. It is expected that officers of all ranks will by their attendance set an example to their men. While we are zealously performing the duties of good citizens and soldiers, we certainly ought not to be inattentive to <u>the higher duties of [Christian] religion.</u> To the distinguished character of patriot, it should be our highest glory to add <u>the more distinguished character of Christian.</u>

31

George Washington shows that living as a Christian is more distinguished than being a patriot. Do you know that our nation is the most unique nation in history and throughout the world? We are the only nation founded as a Christian nation from the start. Other nations converted to be a Christian nation and some nations have allowed their covenant to be broken to their demise. Americans today also need our foundation of Jesus Christ and the Holy Bible. Because of the strong Christian faith of our Founding Fathers, there are too many God endorsements that can be put in any book. Have you asked: Why are some rewriting the USA's history without God? And why is the history of the USA–the greatest nation in the world–being hidden from Americans? If so, ask God how you can help children and every American know the truth. Perhaps, you can have the children and others you know read this book? John Adams said:

The general principles on which the fathers achieved independence were the general principles of Christianity... I will avow that I then believed, and now believe, that those general principles of Christianity are as eternal and immutable as the existence and attributes of God...

---

[1] *USA NEWS 1, http://www.USANews1.com/Covenant*
[2] *Yale Law School, http://avalon.law.yale.edu/17th_century/va01.asp*
[3] *The Enduring Legacy of the First Landing, Doug Phillips, WND,*
   http://www.wnd.com/index.php/index.php?fa=PAGE.printable&pageId=41327
[4] *http://www.vagenweb.org/hening/vol02-13.htm*
[5] *From the Book of General Laws, The Americans, McDougall Littell Inc., http://*
   www.rialto.k12.ca.us/rhs/planetwhited/AP%20PDF%20Docs/Unit%201/Plymo1.pdf
[6] *Faith of Our Founding Fathers, Tim LaHaye (Wolgemuth & Hyatt, Publishers,*
   Inc., 1987), page 103
[7] *http://www.loc.gov/exhibits/religion/rel06-2.html*
[8] *Christian News Update, http://www.ChristianNewsUpdate.com/ChristianNation*

3
The Majority of the USA Are Christians

Father,

We thank You that the USA is Your Christian

nation.

In Jesus' name. Amen.

81% American Majority "believe Jesus Christ is the Son of God who came to earth and died for our sins"
Rasmussen Reports, 2010

If someone told you that Christians outnumber everyone else in the USA, would you believe it? The ungodly try to hide that Christians are the *majority of Americans*. No other group is a close second. The problem is if the Christian majority is silent. Jesus, the apostles and our Founding Fathers show us that God calls us to speak boldly for Him. Is there a way you can stand up for Christ (Romans 1:16)?

81% Believe Jesus Christ

2010 polling reveals 81% of American adults "believe Jesus Christ is the Son of God who came to earth and died for our sins" (Rasmussen Reports). If this number goes up to 100% or down to 51%, the majority of Americans believe Jesus and the Gospel message. Gallop found 81% and 78%

Christians Greatly Outnumber All Others In the USA

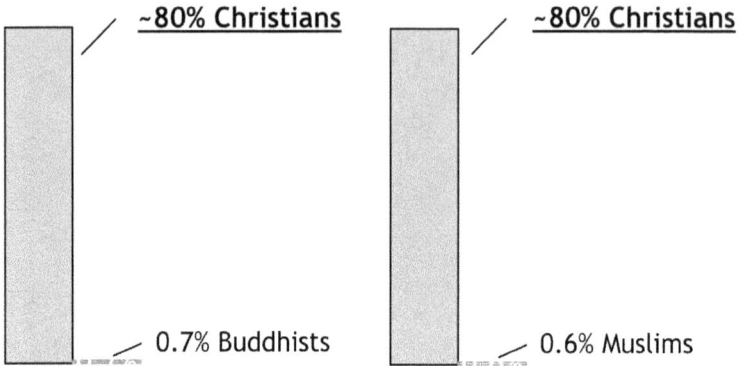

~80% Christians

0.7% Buddhists

~80% Christians

0.6% Muslims

Percentage of USA Who Are Christians Compared to Others
poll data: Rasmussen Reports, 2010, PEW Forum, 2008, Gallop, 2008

Christians (2008, 2009). As you see Christians greatly outnumber all others. But some media doesn't look at Americans the way God does, seeing Christians and non-Christians. Instead, they fall for the devil's scheme to create divisions. Dividing Christians with unBiblical terms such as "right," "left," "centrist" and others is not from God.

Additionally, 92% of American adults celebrate Christmas in their family (Rasmussen Reports, 2010). Christmas and Thanksgiving are government holidays. So why have some promulgated things about small groups like atheists, Muslims and others that often oppose our Founding Fathers' laws and beliefs? Shouldn't the news and businesses share Jesus' hope? Shouldn't businesses promote our nation's Christian faith? It is Christians who won the American Revolution. Do you know that the city of Chicago by itself is larger than all the Muslims in the USA added together? Christians outnumber everyone in America. Look how significant this truth of Christians in the USA is graphically. There is no comparison.

81% Believe Jesus Christ is the Son of God...

- <u>Largest Majority</u> of USA
- Unifying Majority of USA

Americans who Believe Jesus Christ

81%

Non-believers

10% 9% — Still Deciding

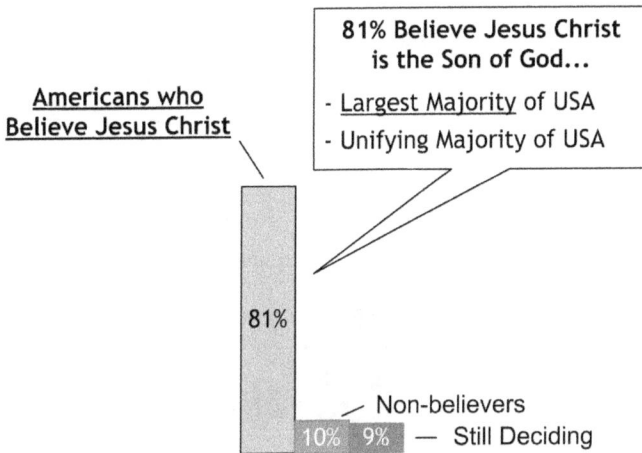

Percentage of USA Who Believe Jesus Christ is the Son of God...

poll data: Adapted from Rasmussen Reports, 2010

We Are Christians, Not Conservatives...

God doesn't want His family divided. Whose country is the USA? By our covenant the USA belongs to God and to Christians. An emphasis to divide the USA by: "Republican," "Democrat," "right," "left," "social conservative," "centrist"... harms us. Being a Christian is superior to all these. Some "conservatives" and "moderates" don't follow Christ. Heathen nations have "moderates". God doesn't accept that. Neither should you. The question is: Are you on the Lord's side? Following Jesus makes the USA strong, not following a "conservative". Jesus said to follow Him, not a "centrist". *This is why we must be called Christians instead of "conservatives".* Christians also outnumber all Republicans and Democrats put together. News and politicians pitting Americans against each other is sin. God calls us to repent. Is Christ divided? Was a political party crucified for you (1 Cor. 1:13)? No. Jesus died for you. That is why Jesus says to follow Him. We honor God by saying, "I am a Christian."

35

Americans who Believe
Jesus Christ...

Christian Nation Majority
- Much Larger than Political Parties

Satan Trys To Divide Christians

Republicans

81%

Other

37% 33.7% 29.3%

Democrats

Christian Faith Is More Important Than Politics

poll data: Rasmussen Reports, 2010 and 2011

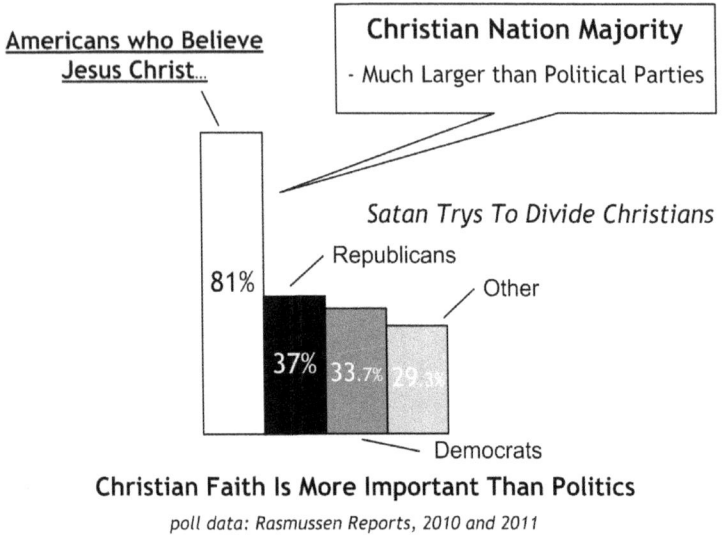

As Christians, our allegiance is to God, not to a political party. Do you agree that being a Christian is more important than anything else? Being a Christian matters now and when Jesus returns. With many Christians involved in the Tea Party, the percentages shown above are likely to change. November 2010 polling shows that the Tea Party is favored eight points higher than Democrats (WND/Wenzel). God's priority for the Tea Party and everyone is to follow Jesus Christ. He is the only one who will save the USA. Americans are to unite our Christian nation. Our nation is united in Christ. Do you want for the USA what Jesus says in the Holy Bible? He warns against dividing Christians. In Matthew 12:25 Jesus says:

[Every] house divided against itself will not stand...

Galatians 5:15 also says, "But if you bite and devour one another, beware lest you be consumed by one another!" Instead, God calls us to be perfectly joined together in the same mind (1 Corinthians 1:10). With brotherly love among Christians, can we agree to follow Jesus Christ (1 Thess. 4:9)?

4

The LORD is the God of the USA and We Are His People

Father,

You are the God of the USA and we are Your
people.

In Jesus' name. Amen.

The USA's covenant with God is the most important part of our nation, other than God. Are you aware how superior our covenant Christian nation is? This is why the first thing our Founding Fathers did was to make covenant with God. Even without our Founding Fathers' covenant, God would still call Christians to covenant the USA to Him today (Psalm 33:12). With our covenant, we declare that the USA chooses the LORD to be our God. As a result, we are God's. He cares for us as our Father. Conversely, efforts to break covenant cause the LORD to withdraw and we lose His favor. Our founding covenant is what sets the USA uniquely above all other nations. As you read this chapter, will you make the decision to affirm our covenant? A prayer follows at the end.

Understand Covenants

First, let's look at what a Christian's covenant and our nation's covenant mean. The LORD is a covenant-making and covenant-keeping God. Even stronger than marriage, God says we are His forever (Gen. 17:2, Deut. 7:9, Luke 22:20).

Every Christian makes a covenant that the LORD (Father, Son and Holy Spirit) is their God and they are His people. Then we live and act as Christians. A Christian's *personal covenant with God* is formed in two parts. There is God's part and your part. A covenant with God is a blood covenant. It has terms and is a binding agreement. God's part is the blood of Jesus on the cross to forgive your sin. Your part is your circumcised heart to love God and to love one another as Jesus loved you (1 John 1:7, Mark 12:30, John 13:34). *Your personal covenant with God is most important to you, for in it you have salvation and have become part of God's family.* God is your Father. It is your responsibility to be saved by confessing with your lips the Lord Jesus and to believe in your heart that God raised Jesus from the dead (Rom. 10:9-10).

Every Christian is part of the body of Christ, including Christians in every nation. *The USA's covenant doesn't replace God's covenant with Abraham and other Biblical covenants.* Our nation's covenant is available as part of Abraham's covenant. Galatians 3:8 says:

And the Scripture, foreseeing that God would justify the Gentiles by faith, preached the gospel to Abraham beforehand, saying, "In you all the nations shall be blessed."

Our focus in this book is on the USA's Covenant with God and its importance to every American. Our covenant that our Founding Fathers gave us continues today. Most Americans know in our hearts that we serve the Lord as His nation. Can you look at the USA from God's perspective? Through our covenant God walks closely with us and He blesses us. He wants to do this. Because God blesses us as His nation, the non-Christians are also blessed. We learn in the covenant of marriage that the unbelievers are sanctified by the believers (1 Cor. 7:14). In other words God treats everyone on the boat with the same grace that Noah had. In contrast, everyone on Jonah's boat got Jonah's storm. So it is in our nation. The unbelievers get the same rain and blessing as those who love God. Similarly, we all get the judgments of God when they come. It is because of the covenant.

Any group of people can agree in covenant with God through Christ Jesus as His people. A family. A city. And a nation–as our Founding Fathers have done. Christians today are in covenant with God across the USA. We agree that the Lord is the God of the USA and that we are His people. You can think of our nation's covenant with God this way: When a Christian husband and wife marry, their family has a special relationship with God. They are still an equal part of the body of Christ. However, they have great blessing by agreeing to serve God together as they walk in unity in Christ. That is how our nation's covenant with God is. As part of the body of Christ, our Founding Fathers chose to covenant our nation to God beginning in 1607. They left Europe to be free of the government limiting the free exercise of Christian faith.

We are one nation under God. Our nation was knowingly covenanted to God. This means that Jesus Christ is Lord of the USA. He is our King. Our laws are based on the Holy Bible; they are obligated to be as our Founding Fathers established. God knows which people, politicians, courts and school boards keep His laws and which don't. As Christians, we are to let God know that we affirm our covenant with Him and that we refuse to give up our covenant under any circumstance. We each are to confess out loud and remind one another: "The USA is a covenant Christian nation." Some don't understand how important this is, but do you?

Also, have you suspected that it takes more than evangelism to make a strong Christian nation? It takes a covenant and Biblical obedience. Jesus said, "Make disciples of all nations... teaching them to observe all things that I have commanded you..." (Matt. 28:19-20). The church is to lead and teach an individual nation God's Word. This is how to make disciples. For example, some other countries have many Christians, but the oppression shows that they haven't yet successfully taken the nation for God. However, the USA was founded as a covenant Christian nation, so God's Kingdom controls the USA, not Satan's darkness. Let's thank God for our faithful church and Bible study leaders. And how many more strong Christians to fill the USA can you believe God for?

The USA's Covenant Relationship With God

The LORD is the God of the USA and We Are His People

① **Keep Covenant** 📖
Give Our Hearts to God
Psalm 33:12, Mark 12:30 & John 13:34

GOD

Jesus' Sacrifice

② **Ask God for Mercy for the USA**
Ezekiel 22:30

GOD'S BLESSINGS

③ **Receive Atonement for Our Sins**
1 John 1:7

To Love God is to Keep the USA From What God Forbids

R E J E C T

Covenant Christian Nation

R E S I S T

Ungodly People (Wicked)
1 Cor. 5:13, Romans 16:17, Titus 3:10, Psalm 15:4 & Psalm 1

The Devil & Sin
James 4:7 & Hebrews 12:4

The USA's Covenant with God

Our nation's covenant with God is summarized as:

The LORD is the God of the USA and we are His people.

We find our covenant in Psalm 33:12. Look at this verse again and see God's promise:

Blessed is the nation whose God is the LORD, the people He has chosen as His own inheritance.

God is saying blessed, which means happy, are the people whose God (*Elohim* – Creator) is the LORD (*Jehovah* – Self-existing One and Covenant keeping God). Then, God says Americans are His own inheritance (people). This is also continued in 2 Corinthians 6:14-16. Notice God says:

Do not be unequally yoked together with unbelievers. For what fellowship has righteousness with lawlessness? And what communion has light with darkness? And what accord has Christ with Belial? Or what part has a believer with an unbeliever? And what agreement has the temple of God with idols?

For our nation this means to not be unequally yoked with unbelievers in relationships and politics, including foreign relationships. Why? We find the answer in 2 Corinthians 6:16:

For you [the USA by covenant] are the temple of the living God [as a people]. As God has said: "I will dwell in them [the hearts of Americans] and walk among them. I will be their God, and they [every American] shall be My people."

What are we to do? God says in 2 Corinthians 6:17-18:

41

> **Therefore "Come out from among them and be separate, says the Lord. Do not touch what is unclean, and I will receive you. I will be a Father to you, and you shall be My sons and daughters, says the LORD Almighty."**

This means the USA is a holy people to God. Each Christian denomination is to stay in agreement with our covenant. Abraham Lincoln affirmed God's unsurpassed blessings from Psalm 33:12 and said:

> **...To recognize the sublime truth, announced in the Holy Scriptures and proven by all history, that those nations only are blessed whose God is the Lord.**

Like George Washington, Abraham Lincoln submitted to God in government. *Notice the word "nations". This again means to endorse combining God and government.* None of our Founding Fathers limited Christians with "separation of church and state". Will you welcome God to rule our Christian nation? Every generation is to affirm our covenant, welcoming the LORD to the USA so we can be in right relationship with God and receive His benefits.

Notice that there are two main parts of our covenant:

1. The LORD is the God of the USA and

2. We are His people.

Our Covenant: The LORD is the God of the USA

The LORD is our God. We recognize His Kingdom and His dominion. He is the object of our love. We reject all other gods, which God calls foreign gods and dumb idols (1 Cor. 12:12). They cannot help us, but offend God. Are you aware that God says it is adultery to have other gods? Judges 10:16 explains that we are to remove all other gods. We see:

So they put away the foreign gods from among them and served the LORD.

As Christians we recognize God's sovereignty over all the works of His creation. We live to serve Him and nothing else. We submit to His Word. But God's enemies "take counsel together... saying, 'Let us break Their [God's] bonds in pieces and cast away Their [God's] cords from us'" (Psalm 2:2-3). Do you know that God delivered our Founding Fathers from tyranny because they served Him? God tells us that He is a jealous God. He will not allow other gods. Will you make a commitment to be faithful to the LORD? Exodus 20:2-7 says:

I am the LORD your God, who brought you... out of the house of bondage. You shall have no other gods before Me. You shall not make for yourself a carved image... you shall not bow down to them nor serve them. For I, the LORD your God, am a jealous God, visiting the iniquity of the fathers upon the children to the third and fourth generations of those who hate Me, but showing mercy to thousands, to those who love Me and keep My commandments...

As your redeemer, Jesus Christ lovingly sacrificed His life on the cross for your sins. He says, "I am the way, the truth, and the life. No one comes to the Father except through Me" (John 14:6). Jesus also explained the devil is the father of lies (John 8:44). Jesus shares that other "religious" beliefs come from the devil, for sins cannot be forgiven without Jesus' blood. Be careful not to be deceived. God says that other gods are a snare. The Hebrew word for snare means a noose by which wild beasts and birds are caught. Exodus 23:33 reads:

For if you serve their gods, it will surely be a snare to you.

Our Covenant: We are His People

The second part of our nation's covenant is we are God's people–His own inheritance (Psalm 33:12). We are comforted that Jesus first chose us to be His (John 15:16). We are God's children through Christ. Every Christian is "accepted in the Beloved" (Ephesians 1:6). As our Father, God forgives, loves, instructs and disciplines us. This is the most important relationship that anyone can have. Jesus bought us with His blood (Rev. 1:5, Acts 20:28). This is true for us as a covenant Christian nation. From our start we have been God's people. 1 Corinthians 6:20 and 2 Corinthians 6:18 say:

> **For you were bought at a price; therefore glorify God in your body and in your spirit, which are God's...**
>
> **I will be a Father to you, and you shall be My sons and daughters, says the LORD Almighty.**

The Covenant Brings God's Blessings

Every Christian should know that our covenant obligates God to fulfill His blessings to us. Three of God's covenant promises are to: 1) forgive, 2) protect and 3) deliver the USA.

Covenant Promises

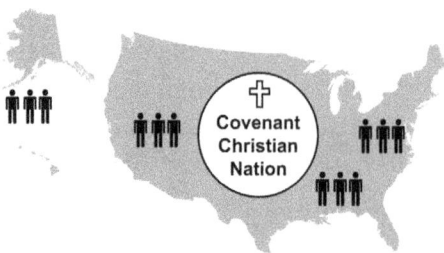

The LORD is the God of the USA and We Are His People

Covenant
Christian
Nation

1) FORGIVENESS
1 John 1:7

2) PROTECTION
Psalm 91

3) DELIVERANCE
Psalm 18

MORE...

Blood Covenant: Jesus' Blood on the Cross + Our Circumcised Hearts

Have you realized that the USA is separated from God in sin without Jesus Christ (John 14:6, 1 Timothy 2:5, Acts 4:12)? This is because without Jesus there is no forgiveness of sin. *However, with covenant God promises to forgive, protect and deliver the USA.* This is important to know. We see God's blessings in His covenant with Abraham. Genesis 17:2 says:

And I will make My covenant between Me and you, and will multiply you exceedingly.

Since Jesus Christ came through this covenant, these blessings apply through Jesus Christ to Christians today.

What is the USA to Do in Covenant?

In Mark 12:30 and John 13:34, Jesus gives us God's commandments for us. We are to fulfill them. We have our part in covenant too. These are God's purpose for the USA.

First Commandment for the USA *(Mark 12:30)*

You shall love the LORD your God with all your heart, with all your soul, with all your mind, and with all your strength.

Let's look at what this means.

With All Your Heart: To love God with all your heart is to love God from the deepest part of you. It means you have no other gods before Him, you do not make and serve idols, you do not take God's name in vain, and you obey what God says in the Holy Bible (Exodus 20:3-11, John 14:21).

With All Your Soul: You love God with all your soul by desiring God. He wants to be your affection. This is loving God with all your emotions and obeying Him. You love what God loves and hate what God hates (Luke 1:46, 1 Peter 1:22).

45

With All Your Mind: To love God with all your mind includes all your thoughts and intents. It is to think about and meditate on God's laws in the Holy Bible (Hebrews 10:16, Ephesians 2:1-3, Philippians 4:8-9).

With All Your Strength: God asks for you to love Him with all your strength. This means with all your power, ability and might. With all your strength and ability you offer your life to God. You serve Him not yourself (1 Peter 4:11).

The USA's Covenant With God ™

The LORD is the God of the USA and We Are His People

1) FORGIVENESS

2) PROTECTION

God's Laws

The LORD dwells with us

Love God
Love One Another

Jesus is King

Covenant Christian Nation

3) DELIVERANCE

4) MORE BLESSINGS

We Love God with All Our Heart, Soul, Mind and Strength (Mark 12:30)

- **Jesus is our King** (Isaiah 33:22, Philippians 2:11, Psalms 47:7-9)

- **We Obey What God Says in the Holy Bible** (2 Timothy 3:16-17)

We Love One Another as Jesus Loved Us (John 13:34)

Second Commandment for the USA (John 13:34)

Love one another; as I have loved you, that you also love one another.

Look at Jesus. Can you see that He loves you perfectly and with joy? He endured the cross to give His life for you and now is interceding for you. He will never leave you. Jesus is faithful to complete the work He began in you. Jesus accepts you perfectly (Ephesians 1:6). By yielding yourself to God, you can love as Jesus loves you. To love one another as Jesus loved us often involves sacrifice. We are to love our Christian family and to love our enemies. This love God asks of us is a daily lifestyle (Romans 5:8, 1 John 3:16, Hebrews 12:2). Ephesians 5:2 says "walk in love".

Covenant Warning

Here are some Biblical truths that may surprise you. While God is merciful, He will not be mocked. God is holy. Do you know that if the USA does not obey our covenant with God, then God warns that He will destroy our nation (Ezekiel 22:30, Malachi 4:6)? To understand this, let's look at Moses. When Moses did not bring his son into covenant by circumcision, we see God was prepared to kill Moses. However, his wife circumcised their son, which spared Moses and his family from God's judgment for breaking covenant (Exodus 4:24-26). This means that in the areas the USA is not obeying God. We must now repent and obey God. When we look at the book of Jeremiah, we see Israel was taken captive for breaking their covenant with God. This is one reason why we can't allow our Christian nation to forsake God.

Our covenant with God is made by Christians. Non-Christians cannot take the USA away from God. Only Christians can allow the USA to be taken away from God, for this is our covenant. God tells us that those who forsake Him, He will forsake. 2 Chronicles 15:2 and 2 Timothy 2:12 say:

47

The LORD is with you while you are with Him. If you seek Him, He will be found by you; but if you forsake Him, He will forsake you.

If we deny Him, He also will deny us.

God's blesses the USA while the USA is with Him, but if we don't walk with Him, then God says He will forsake our nation. Will you tell God you welcome Him to the USA?

A Covenant with God Heals Great Turmoil

When the church, especially the men, do not take responsibility for the USA, then there is national turmoil. This happened in Judah. Notice 2 Chronicles 15:3-6 says:

For a long time Israel has been without the true God, without a teaching priest, and without law; but when in their trouble they turned to the LORD God of Israel, and sought Him, He was found by them. And in those times there was no peace to the one who went out, nor to the one who came in, but great turmoil was on all the inhabitants of the lands. So nation was destroyed by nation, and city by city, for God troubled them with every adversity.

Without the men teaching God's Word, then the people had great turmoil. What did Judah do to stop the turmoil? The next few verses show that King Asa took courage, removed the abominable idols from all the land, restored the altar, gathered the people, gave a sacrifice for their sin and they re-affirmed covenant to seek God with all their heart and with all their soul (2 Chronicles 15:7-12). Those who would not seek the LORD God they put to death as under the law of the Old Testament (Deut. 13). As Christians today, we put away evil people differently. We forbid them to be involved in the church and our nation unless they repent. God tells pastors and every Christian to obey Him in this (1 Cor. 5:13). What was the result for Judah? 2 Chronicles 15:15 and 19 show:

> **And all Judah rejoiced at the oath, for they had sworn with all their heart and sought Him with all their soul; and He was found by them, and the LORD gave them rest all around... there was no war until the thirty-fifth year of the reign of Asa.**

God gave them rest and stopped wars because they turned to Him. The same is true with the USA. We see that great turmoil comes when God is not sought and obeyed, but when our nation turns to God, He gives peace. Asa's name means "healer". He is acknowledged for removing those who did not stop being obscene. 2 Chronicles 15:16 reads:

> **Also he removed Maachah, the mother of Asa the king, from being queen mother, because she had made an obscene image of Asherah; and Asa cut down her obscene image, then crushed and burned it by the brook Kidron.**

However, King Asa did not remove everything against God, which could be why Israel only had temporary peace.

Someone may say, "But what about the non-Christians in the USA? How can we force them to follow God's laws?" The answer to this is the USA is a Christian nation. If a person is not a Christian, they know that we are a Christian nation. We have been a Christian nation in covenant for over four hundred years. If someone does not want to live in our Christian nation, then they shouldn't be here. Christians can't allow anyone to lead us away from God. That is like letting a stranger tell your family what to do. You wouldn't let that happen and neither can we let the ungodly tell us what to do.

Someone else may say, "How can you require me to follow Christian laws?" The answer to this is our nation was founded with Christian laws. George Washington, John Adams, John Jay and our Founding Fathers made our Christian laws. The real question is: Why is that person unthankful and opposing our Founding Fathers and God?

Do you see how our nation can only be blessed by serving God? As Abraham Lincoln shared, this is proven by God's Word and history. What God wants is that we work diligently to make the USA a strong Christian nation. As a Christian, are you ready to exalt God and welcome Him to the USA? Now, will you affirm our covenant with God and live it? Pray:

The USA's Covenant With God Prayer™

Father,

As a Christian nation dedicated to You, we affirm our covenant:

- **You, the LORD, are the God of the USA and we are Your people. Jesus is our King. We obey what You say in the Holy Bible.**

- **We love You with all our heart, soul, mind and strength.**

- **We love one another as Jesus loved us.**

- **We ask You to forgive our sins by Jesus' sacrifice.**

In Jesus' name. Amen. *Psalm 33:12, Mark 12:30, John 13:34, 2 Chronicles 15:12, 1 John 1:7*

See www.USAChristianMinistries.com for tools.

Permission is given to reprint and pray The USA's Covenant with God™ in handouts, articles and on TV and radio provided the prayer is given for free and includes a reference to USAChristianMinistries.com. For other uses contact USA Christian Ministries to inquire about permission.

5
The Benefits of
Our Christian Nation

Father,

We thank You for Your blessings for the USA.

In Jesus' name. Amen.

D o you know that only a Christian nation can be blessed abundantly by God? This is because Jesus is the door every nation must go through to see the Kingdom of God. Jesus said, "I am the door" (John 10:9). God's uncommon blessings come through Jesus Christ. After we enter in, as the USA has done by covenant, we live as a nation for God. Have you realized that the USA has been set above all nations for our obeying God? Deut. 28:1-2 reveals:

> **Now it shall come to pass, if you diligently obey the voice of the LORD your God, to observe carefully all His commandments which I command you today, that the LORD your God will set you high above all nations of the earth.**

> **And all these blessings shall come upon you and overtake you, because you obey the voice of the LORD your God...**

Obeying God Makes Strong Families & Brings Prosperity
As Explained in Eph. 5:22-33, Deuteronomy 28, Leviticus 26...

1 OBEYING GOD

Love God
Love One Another

God's Holy Ways
• Christian Nation Covenant
• Include God in Home & Government
• Christian Prayer and
  the Holy Bible in Schools
• Pro-Life Nation - End Abortion
• Christian Families
  1 Man + 1 Woman Lifelong Marriage
• Love One Another
  As Jesus Loved Us
• All God's Commands...

2 BRINGS GOD'S BLESSINGS
ACROSS THE USA

Blessings
• God Dwells With Us • Strong Families
  Lev. 26:11-12   Eph. 5:22-33
• Prosperity & Wealth • No Debt
  Deut. 28:4-5,8,11-12   Deut. 28:12
• Security & Protection • Peace
  Deut. 28:7, Lev. 26:7-8   Lev. 26:6
• No Terrorism   • Freedom
  Deut. 28:7, Lev. 26:6   2 Cor. 3:17
• Love and More...
  John 13:35, Deut. 28:1-14, Lev. 26:1-13

Christian Nation Blessings

Blessings of Our Christian Nation (the USA)

George Washington, John Adams, Abraham Lincoln and our Founding Fathers believed God blesses our nation for obeying Him. For example, George Washington told the USA:

> **...to acknowledge our many and great obligations to Almighty God and to implore Him to continue and confirm the blessings we experience.**

Are you thankful for how God has blessed our nation? Look at the blessings God gives below. Can you see how He gave these blessings throughout our history? God wants to give the same to us today (Deut. 28:1-14, Lev. 26:1-13...).

Blessing 1   **God Walks with Us and Dwells with the USA**
Deuteronomy 28:9 promises, "The LORD will establish you as a holy people to Himself, just as He has sworn to you, if you keep the commandments of the LORD your God and walk in His ways." When the USA welcomes God, He dwells

with us. Leviticus 26:11-12 says, "I will set My tabernacle among you, and My soul shall not abhor you. I will walk among you and be your God, and you shall be My people." With Jesus in our hearts, our nation becomes God's tabernacle.

Blessing 2 **Strong Families**
When a nation includes God and the Holy Bible in families, schools, courts and the government, then the families of the nation are strong. This is because building on the foundation of God's Word, godliness, sexual purity and one man and one woman lifetime marriage makes strong families (Eph 5:22-33, Prov. 22:6...). Deuteronomy 28:3 says, "Blessed shall you be in the city, and blessed shall you be in the country."

Blessing 3 **Prosperity and Wealth for the USA**
Obeying God has prospered the USA. Deuteronomy 28:4-5, 8 and 11-12 assure, "Blessed shall be the fruit of your body, the produce of your ground and the increase of your herds...," "The LORD will command the blessing on you..." and "...the LORD will grant you plenty of goods... The LORD will open to you His good treasure, the heavens, to give the rain to your land in its season, and to bless all the work of your hand."

Blessing 4 **God's Protection, National Security and Peace**
Protection comes from God. He gave the USA the number one military for obeying Him. Deuteronomy 28:7 promises, "The LORD will cause your enemies who rise against you to be defeated before your face..." The 1777 Georgia Preamble confirms, "We, the people of Georgia, relying upon the protection and guidance of Almighty God." Leviticus 26:6 says, "I will give peace in the land..." God gives peace.

Blessing 5 **Freedom for the People**
Freedom is the fruit of obeying God. It is God's blessing. Our Declaration of Independence acknowledges freedom comes

from God with: "they are endowed by their Creator with certain unalienable Rights... Liberty..." *Only a Christian nation has freedom.* This is because God is welcome and "where the Spirit of the Lord is there is liberty" *(2 Cor. 3:17).* The New England Articles of Confederation 1643 also say freedom is from God with: "We all came... to enjoy the liberties of the Gospel". New York's Constitution declares: "grateful to Almighty God for our freedom..." Two weeks before signing the Declaration, John Adams said, "Statesmen... may plan and speculate for liberty, but it is [Christian] religion and morality alone, which can establish the principles upon which freedom can securely stand." Leviticus 25:10 is written on the Liberty bell to proclaim God's freedom.

Blessing 6   Honesty, Integrity, Morals and Justice
God blesses a Christian nation with virtue and integrity, for "righteousness and justice are the foundation of His throne". To have God is to have justice (Psalm 97:2, Mark 10:18).

Blessing 7   A Nation of Love
Only a Christian nation has God's love. Jesus says, "By this all will know that you are My disciples, if you have love for one another" (John 13:35).

Blessing 8   The USA Lends to Nations and Doesn't Borrow
God promises, "You shall lend to many nations, but you shall not borrow" (Deut. 28:12). The USA having so much money earlier is because of obeying God, making His laws our laws.

Blessing 9   A Giving / Benevolent Nation
Our nation is the most benevolent nation in history because of our Christian faith (Mark 9:41, Matthew 28:19-20).

Blessing 10   United–the USA is a Christian Family
The USA is united in Christ. We are a family. Ephesians 4:3 says, "Endeavoring to keep the unity of the Spirit..."

Blessing 11   **Other Nations Will Fear the USA**

Deuteronomy 28:10 shows, "Then all peoples of the earth shall see that you are called by the name of the LORD, and they shall be afraid of you." With this respect, our nation has seen God's supernatural favor and protection.

Blessing 12   **Set High Above All Nations of the Earth**

The USA became the number one nation in the world by knowing Jesus (Psalm 91:14, Matthew 6:33). For the reward of obeying God Deuteronomy 28:1 promises, "The LORD your God will set you high above all nations of the earth."

There are more blessings too.

God Calls the USA to Serve Him

With God giving so many blessings to the obedient, it is wise to look at people how God does. Malachi 3:18 explains:

Then you shall again discern between the righteous and the wicked, between one who serves God and one who does not serve Him.

God describes two types of people: The righteous and the wicked. Our nation is blessed when we see people how God does. God's perspective is shown throughout His Word as:

- Children of God and children of the devil (1 John 3:10)
- Sons of the day and sons of the night (1 Thess. 5:5)
- Sons of light and sons of darkness (1 Thess. 5:5)
- Saint and sinner (1 Corinthians 6:1, Luke 15:7)
- Sheep and goats (Matthew 25:33)
- Wheat and tares (Matthew 13:30)
- The righteous and the wicked (Mal. 3:18, Gen. 18:23)
- The just and the unjust (Acts 24:15) and
- The one who serves God and the one who does not serve Him (Malachi 3:18)

It is the same with nations. When God looks at a nation, He sees only two types of nations: A nation in covenant with Him and an ungodly nation that hasn't made a covenant. He expects our nation to obey Him as His people (John 14:21).

God Blesses the Nation that Serves Him

Don't you feel good being a Christian? Now, notice that God seeks to dwell with us because He cares for us? In the Old Testament, Moses built a tabernacle in which God would dwell. But after Jesus' sacrifice for sin on the cross, each person calling on Jesus to be saved becomes the tabernacle of God. Through Jesus Christ's atonement we are God's dwelling place (1 Cor. 3:16). Christians are to be holy and separate to God. God wants His tabernacle of people to fill across the USA. 2 Corinthians 6:16-17 say:

> **For you are the temple of the living God. As God has said: "I will dwell in them and walk among them. I will be their God, and they shall be My people."**

Now, let's ask: What are God's best plans for the USA? *God's will is for the USA to be a strong Christian nation.* A Christian nation is a nation in covenant with God, daily living for God and blessed by Him above other nations. Our nation follows Jesus Christ. We can't make other nations follow Him. They each have to decide to walk in covenant with God themselves. Can you see that the Biblical teachings applying to disciples, family and church, also apply to our nation? When Jesus sent his apostles out He told them to "make disciples of every nation." This means the USA is to fully make disciples of the USA. He also said He would give His blessing to a nation bearing the fruits thereof (Matthew 21:43). Let's do everything that Jesus wants in the USA.

56

What are the main reasons why God wants the USA to be a strong Christian nation? Here are ten truths to teach in our government and in every church, school and homeschool:

Why God Wants the USA a Strong Christian Nation

1. **God Expects Nations to Follow Him**
   God says to make the LORD our God (Psalm 33:12).

2. **God Wants a Tabernacle in Our Nation**
   The Holy Spirit seeks to dwell in each heart as a tabernacle across our nation (1 Cor. 3:16, Lev. 26:11).

3. **God Wants Fellowship with the USA**
   God's ultimate intention for our nation is that we are His people (Psalm 33:12, Lev. 26:12).

4. **God Seeks to Fill our Nation With Himself**
   Jesus is the Head of the church and He wants His body (church) to fill the USA (Ephesians 1:22, 4:15).

5. **Jesus Said: Make Disciples of the USA**
   One of God's greatest desires is for whole nations to be His disciples who obey Him (Matthew 28:18-20).

6. **Our Nation is to Seek First the Kingdom of God**
   God tells the USA to "seek first the Kingdom of God and His righteousness" (Matthew 6:33).

7. **The USA Can Only Come to God Through Jesus**
   God wants to redeem each nation. Jesus is the way to the Father. Jesus' death forgives our nation's sins. No nation can come to God except through Jesus (John 14:6).

8. **God Desires to Bless the USA**
   God wants our nation to be blessed. Only a Christian nation has God's true blessings (Psalm 33:12).

9. **Our Christian Nation Glorifies God**
"All nations whom You have made shall come and worship before You, O Lord, and shall glorify Your name" (Psalm 89:6).

10. **Jesus Came to Give Americans Life**
God wants the USA to have life abundantly, being free from sin, Satan and the world (John 10:9-10).

More Blessings Than We Can Write

Can you see that God's best plans for our nation are to have every American as His family? He wants to dwell with us by dwelling in our hearts. Do you see that it is sin for any American to not want a strong Christian nation where God fills the USA (Matthew 28:19-20)? Will you surrender your life to God, letting Him know that, through Jesus, you give yourself, your family and our nation to Him?

Our Founding Fathers knew that God was our source of blessings. Look for the words "nations' and "country" in these quotes below. This reaffirms to include God in government. John Adams said with wisdom:

...the safety and prosperity of nations ultimately and essentially depend on the protection and the blessing of Almighty God.

Daniel Webster reminded us:

If we abide by the principles taught in the Bible, our country will go on prospering and to prosper.

When the USA obeys God, we have His blessings, which include: prosperity and wealth, freedom, strong families, love and a government that cares for the people. Can you pray for the USA to obey God in all things (Galatians 6:7-8)?

6

The Cause of Economic Loss and Losing Freedom

Father,

We beseech You to pardon our national and other transgressions, as George Washington also prayed for the USA.

In Jesus' name. Amen.

Some Americans don't understand that God says our national sins are the reason for economic loss and losing freedom. Our Founding Fathers believed this and it is one reason why they had days of prayer and fasting with repentance. Until we deal with the sin issues today, God says that our nation's problems won't go away. Continuing to disobey God only makes things worse. Are you ready to gain God's blessings and to overcome our problem's God's way?

Why Sin Blocks God's Blessings

Each American should look at what goes on in the USA. Why is it that "if we just got a 'smart person' to fix the economy" doesn't work? What causes our borders to not be secure? What causes large debt and corruption? We will now show that disobeying God is the cause. To solve our nation's problems, God tells the USA to turn from our sin as a nation. Some may think sin isn't a big deal, but Galatians 6:7-8 says:

59

> **Do not be deceived, God is not mocked; for whatever a man sows, that he will also reap. For he who sows to his flesh will of the flesh reap corruption, but he who sows to the Spirit will of the Spirit reap everlasting life.**

Financial loss, national debt, foreigners rising up and endless wars are the consequence of a nation's sin (Deuteronomy 28:15-68). Without God's blessing, the economy, government, military and our nation suffer. Have you suspected that a nation's sin results in curses for that nation? God says this again and again. For example, economic loss came because of Saul's sin. 2 Samuel 21:1 says:

> **Now there was a famine... and David inquired of the LORD. And the LORD answered, "It is because of Saul and his bloodthirsty house, because he killed the Gibeonites."**

Another example is the plague that resulted in 70,000 men dying in Israel when David disobeyed God (2 Samuel 24). There are many other examples such as Manasseh who brought foreign gods, sorcery, shedding of innocent blood and sexual sin to Judah. Because the nation didn't separate from and reject Manasseh, the sins brought plunderers and turning Jerusalem upside down until it was destroyed. Do you see that God is not mocked? 2 Kings 21:11-13 say:

> **Because Manasseh... has done these abominations (he has acted more wickedly than all the Amorites who were before him, and has also made Judah sin with his idols), therefore thus says the LORD God of Israel: 'Behold, I am bringing such calamity upon Jerusalem and Judah, that... ears will tingle... I will wipe Jerusalem as one wipes a dish, wiping it and turning it upside down.'**

Disobeying God is Why the Economy Declines and Freedoms Are Removed

As Explained in Galatians 6:7-8, Deuteronomy 28 and Leviticus 26

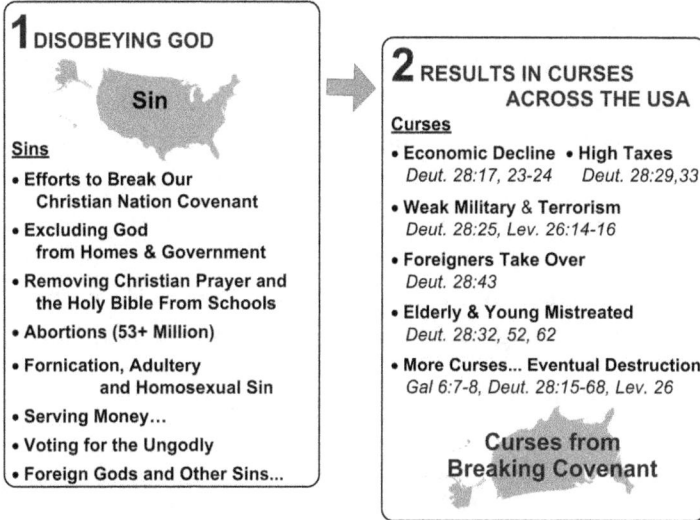

1 DISOBEYING GOD

Sin

Sins

- Efforts to Break Our Christian Nation Covenant
- Excluding God from Homes & Government
- Removing Christian Prayer and the Holy Bible From Schools
- Abortions (53+ Million)
- Fornication, Adultery and Homosexual Sin
- Serving Money...
- Voting for the Ungodly
- Foreign Gods and Other Sins...

2 RESULTS IN CURSES ACROSS THE USA

Curses

- **Economic Decline** • **High Taxes**
  Deut. 28:17, 23-24   Deut. 28:29,33
- **Weak Military & Terrorism**
  Deut. 28:25, Lev. 26:14-16
- **Foreigners Take Over**
  Deut. 28:43
- **Elderly & Young Mistreated**
  Deut. 28:32, 52, 62
- **More Curses... Eventual Destruction**
  Gal 6:7-8, Deut. 28:15-68, Lev. 26

Curses from
Breaking Covenant

The Root Issues Must Be Removed For Success

Before we look at curses in more detail, it is important to understand that to end high taxes, loss of freedom and other curses, God calls for national repentance. God's Word says these curses are caused by sin. *Sin is the root issue* that must be removed to end the curses. This is why efforts to remove the fruit issues, or curses, alone can't succeed. That is like trimming a weed. Unless you remove the root it grows back.

God calls us to repent from sin and not just want lower taxes or not to be in debt like non-Christians do. Think about it. God is holy. Do you think God's priority is for the USA not to be taxed as much or to have freedom, but then not to live in holiness and to exclude God from our homes and government? No. This is why the same anger that has driven Americans to oppose government corruption should wisely be

61

focused to remove the sin from the USA. Otherwise, God sees that we just want money and "freedom" but not Him. God cares about our finances. He wants us to have true Christian freedom. But blessings come from obeying Him. Have you noticed that our Founding Fathers said this? To have success, everyone concerned with corruption should focus their efforts to call for national repentance of the root sin issues. Otherwise, God says the corruption will not end. *This is why Christians will save the USA but "conservatives" can't.* The First Commandment is to love God not the economy and freedom. When we love God by repentance, He promises to give His blessings (2 Chron. 7:14, Judges 3:9, John 14:21).

God Says Sin is the Cause for Government Corruption

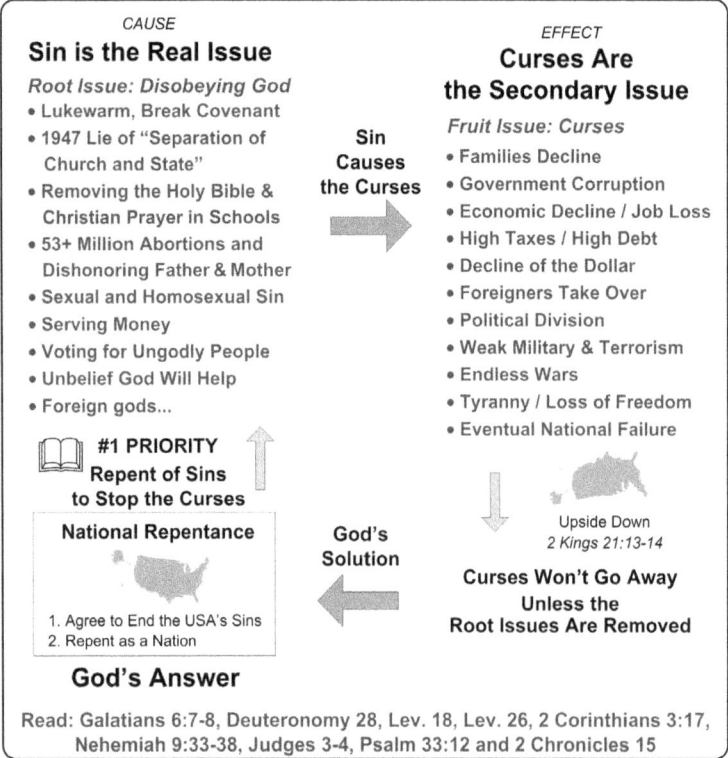

CAUSE
Sin is the Real Issue

Root Issue: Disobeying God
- Lukewarm, Break Covenant
- 1947 Lie of "Separation of Church and State"
- Removing the Holy Bible & Christian Prayer in Schools
- 53+ Million Abortions and Dishonoring Father & Mother
- Sexual and Homosexual Sin
- Serving Money
- Voting for Ungodly People
- Unbelief God Will Help
- Foreign gods...

Sin Causes the Curses

EFFECT
Curses Are the Secondary Issue

Fruit Issue: Curses
- Families Decline
- Government Corruption
- Economic Decline / Job Loss
- High Taxes / High Debt
- Decline of the Dollar
- Foreigners Take Over
- Political Division
- Weak Military & Terrorism
- Endless Wars
- Tyranny / Loss of Freedom
- Eventual National Failure

#1 PRIORITY
Repent of Sins to Stop the Curses

National Repentance

1. Agree to End the USA's Sins
2. Repent as a Nation

God's Solution

Upside Down
2 Kings 21:13-14

Curses Won't Go Away Unless the Root Issues Are Removed

God's Answer

Read: Galatians 6:7-8, Deuteronomy 28, Lev. 18, Lev. 26, 2 Corinthians 3:17, Nehemiah 9:33-38, Judges 3-4, Psalm 33:12 and 2 Chronicles 15

Biblically Understand High Taxes and Debt

High taxes and a nation's debt are plundering. Plundering happens when there is sin. Sin comes when the men do not teach the people the Holy Bible and do not ask God to forgive the sins of the people. By obeying God's laws, the USA was founded with no personal taxes. Americans were more blessed earlier. However, the Holy Bible explains that because of our nation's sin our money is being plundered with high taxes and debt. We have seen many taxes like "inheritance tax" that our Founding Fathers never wanted. 2 Kings 17:15-20 say:

> **[Israel and Judah] rejected His statutes and His covenant that He had made with their fathers... they followed idols, became idolaters, and went after the nations who were all around them, concerning whom the LORD had charged them that they should not do like them... And they caused their sons and daughters to pass through the fire [to kill them like abortion]... and sold themselves to do evil in the sight of the LORD, to provoke Him to anger... And the LORD rejected all the descendants of Israel, afflicted them, and delivered them into the hand of plunderers...**

Nehemiah 9:34-37 explains that forsaking God, results in lost freedom. It tells us:

> **Neither our kings nor our princes, our priests nor our fathers, have kept Your law, nor heeded Your commandments and Your testimonies... Nor did they turn from their wicked works. Here we are, servants today! And the land that You gave to our fathers, to eat its fruit and its bounty, here we are, servants in it! And it yields much increase to the kings You have set over us, because of our sins;**

Also they have dominion over our bodies and our cattle at their pleasure; And we are in great distress.

A nation's sins are what lead to the oppression of Socialism and Communism, for God's freedom is removed.

The Truth about Curses

Jesus Christ came to "proclaim liberty to the captives... to set at liberty those who are oppressed", but if He is not followed then there is captivity and oppression from sin (Luke 4:18). Expanding more details from Galatians 6:7-8, it is helpful to read Deuteronomy 28:15-68 and Leviticus 26:14-38 to understand what God says about curses for a nation. Deuteronomy 28:15 and Leviticus 26:14-16 say:

But it shall come to pass, if you do not obey the voice of the LORD your God... all these curses will come upon you and overtake you...

But... if you despise My statutes, or if your soul abhors My judgments, so that you do not perform all My commandments, but break My covenant, I also will do this to you...

Now, let's look at the curses that come from disobedience:

Curse 1 Government Corruption / Cursed Nation
Government corruption comes as a result of a nation disobeying God, despising His statutes, abhorring His judgments and not performing His commandments (Lev. 26:14-16). Leviticus 26:17 says, "Those who hate you shall reign over you..." Deuteronomy 28:16 shows, "Cursed shall you be in the city, and cursed shall you be in the country."

Curse 2   Economic Decline / Famine in the USA

Deuteronomy 28:17, 23-24 say, "Cursed shall be your basket and your kneading bowl" and "...your heavens which are over your head shall be bronze, and the earth which is under you shall be iron. The LORD will change the rain of your land to powder and dust... until you are destroyed."

Curse 3   Weak Military / Endless Wars

Deuteronomy 28:25 warns, "The LORD will cause you to be defeated before your enemies; you shall go out one way against them and flee seven ways before them; and you shall become troublesome to all the kingdoms of the earth."

Curse 4   Terrorism

The reason the USA hasn't won terrorism is because it is a curse for our nation's sin. Leviticus 26:16 says, "But if you... break My covenant... I will even appoint terror over you..."

Curse 5   Foreigners Take Over / Aliens

Deuteronomy 28:43 warns, "The alien who is among you shall rise higher and higher above you, and you shall come down lower and lower." God says that multi-languages are a result of not seeking Him, as at the tower of Babel. The real reason for foreigners rising is because the USA has disobeyed God, for example with abortion and sexual sins. Only 2.98% of illegal aliens were deported (2009). Leviticus 26:38 says, "You shall perish among the nations, and the land of your enemies shall eat you up."

Curse 6   Our Money Plundered / High Taxes

Deuteronomy 28:29 and 33 say, "... you shall not prosper in your ways; you shall be only oppressed and plundered continually, and no one shall save you" and "A nation whom you have not known shall eat the fruit of your land..."

Curse 7   **Sickness, Plagues... Non-Christian "Healthcare"**
Deuteronomy 28:21-22 and 27-28 declare, "The LORD will make the plague cling to you until He has consumed you from the land which you are going to possess. The LORD will strike you with consumption, with fever, with inflammation, with severe burning fever, with the sword, with scorching, and with mildew; they shall pursue you until you perish" and "The LORD will strike you with the boils of Egypt, with tumors, with the scab, and with the itch, from which you cannot be healed..." Disobedience leads to poor "healthcare".

Curse 8   **The USA Deceived by Foreign Gods (Satan)**
Deuteronomy 28:36 warns, "The LORD will bring you and the king whom you set over you to a nation which neither you nor your fathers have known, and there you shall serve other gods—wood and stone..." The curse of foreign gods is because of turning away from the true God.

Curse 9   **Other Nations Will Mock the USA**
Deuteronomy 28:37 shows, "And you shall become an astonishment, a proverb, and a byword among all nations..." Americans are not as respected as before because some Christians and churches haven't opposed recent sins, including voting for the ungodly and not fearing God.

Curse 10   **The USA Borrows and Goes into High Debt**
Deuteronomy 28:44 shows, "[Foreigners] shall lend to you, but you shall not lend to him; he shall be the head, and you shall be the tail." This explains why there is such high debt.

Curse 11   **Removal of God's Anointing—Failed Businesses**
Deuteronomy 28:40 warns, "You shall have olive trees throughout all your territory, but you shall not anoint yourself with the oil; for your olives shall drop off."

Curse 12   **Elderly and Young Mistreated**
Families declining are from disobeying God (Galatians 6:7-8). But weak families are only the beginning as Deuteronomy 28:49-50 warns, "The LORD will bring a nation against you from afar, from the end of the earth, as swift as the eagle flies, a nation whose language you will not understand, a nation of fierce countenance, which does not respect the elderly nor show favor to the young."

Curse 13   **People Will Be Hostile to Each Other**
The curses get worse as sin and Satan take over instead of God and holiness. Are you seeing why sin must be dealt with and not ignored? Deuteronomy 28:54-57 warn, "The sensitive and very refined man among you will be hostile toward his brother, toward the wife of his bosom, and toward the rest of his children whom he leaves behind, so that he will not give any of them the flesh of his children whom he will eat... The tender and delicate woman among you, who would not venture to set the sole of her foot on the ground because of her delicateness and sensitivity, will refuse to the husband of her bosom, and to her son and her daughter..."

Curse 14   **Taken Captive into a Foreign Land**
Deuteronomy 28:32, 52 and 62 warn, "Your sons and your daughters shall be given to another people, and your eyes shall look and fail with longing for them all day long; and there shall be no strength in your hand...," "They shall besiege you at all your gates until your high and fortified walls, in which you trust, come down throughout all your land..." and "You shall be left few in number, whereas you were as the stars of heaven in multitude, because you would not obey the voice of the LORD your God."

There are other curses too. Now, let's look at the magnitude of curses and see what God says causes them to multiply.

Seven Times Greater Judgments

Do you know that God says the curses get worse by factors of seven when a nation doesn't repent? This means that if there isn't national repentance, then God says the curses will get worse by a factor of seven. Leviticus 26:23-24 shows, "And if by these things you are not reformed by Me, but walk contrary to Me, then I also will walk contrary to you, and I will punish you yet seven times for your sins." Increasing judgments seven times occurs four times in Lev. 26.

The Dangers of Breaking Covenant

Have you suspected that corruption, terrorism, foreigners rising up and other curses are a sign and a wonder? In God's mercy the curses are a warning to seek Him and to turn from wicked ways. Deuteronomy 28:45-48, 58 and 63 tell us:

> **Moreover all these curses shall come upon you and pursue and overtake you, until you are destroyed, because you did not obey the voice of the LORD your God, to keep His commandments and His statutes which He commanded you.**

> **And they shall be upon you for a sign and a wonder, and on your descendants forever.**

> **Because you did not serve the LORD your God with joy and gladness of heart, for the abundance of everything, therefore you shall serve your enemies, whom the LORD will send against you...**

> **And it shall be, that just as the LORD rejoiced over you to do you good and multiply you, so the LORD will rejoice over you to destroy you...**

Notice "Because you did not serve the LORD your God with joy and gladness of heart..." God calls us to love Him.

68

Sin Means American Families Suffer

Can we agree that God has better plans for the USA? He doesn't want our families and nation to have these troubles. God sees the following as recent efforts to break covenant:

1947: Lie of "Separation of Church and State"

An activist court made the lie of "separation of church and state" in 1947. They ruled not only in opposition to the Constitution, but also in opposition to our Founding Fathers, history and God as will be explained. That court falsely makes George Washington, John Adams, Thomas Jefferson and Abraham Lincoln criminals as the USA has on purpose combined Christian churches into our government. This bad law is not the intent of God or the USA.

1954: Pastors Limited by 501(c)(3) Organizations

If you are a pastor, can you pray how you can speak truthfully for God politically with or without a 501(c)(3)? 501(c)(3) organizations didn't exist until 1954. What has been the result? Since a 501(c)(3) says it limits a pastor's speech, it makes a weaker church, leading to corruption in the USA. Can you imagine Paul or Peter limiting their speech or serving the state and not God? No. That is why neither Jesus, nor our Founding Fathers had non-profit organizations. The real issue is anyone opposing our Founding Fathers and our Christian Constitution that tells us the opposite. The Constitution says:

> **Congress shall make no law... prohibiting the free exercise [of Christian religion]...**

Some may say, "But what about the government benefits?" The answer is: Christians aren't to limit the Gospel for government benefits. To love God is also to warn people to avoid politicians and "laws" that disobey God and lead the USA into sin. This is a challenging issue but let's pray how we can be faithful to Christ. Perhaps some ministries can also branch out with a new ministry that isn't limited? And others can speak truthfully for God with a 501(c)(3) as the First Amendment prohibits limiting Christians? Pastors should seek God on what He desires. I also want to share what God revealed to me regarding tax deductions. I realized Biblically that what I give to God is all God's. In other words, I am not supposed to get a tax deduction. So when I give to a ministry that doesn't give tax write-offs, I automatically give everything to God. And if I give to a ministry that has a tax write-off, then I also give the tax-deduction I get back to God.

1962: 355 Years of Prayer in Schools Stopped

While Christian prayer has been in schools since 1607, an activist court in 1962 removed a blessing prayer. Why would a court not want God's blessing? As a result, school scores are down–and child abuse and crimes are up. The prayer was:

Almighty God, we acknowledge our depend- ence upon thee, and we beg Thy blessings upon us, our parents, our teachers and our Country.

1963: Activist Court Removes Prayer & Bible from School

An activist court chose to remove prayer and Bible reading from our schools in 1963. Again, this is opposing our nation's history of training American children in the Lord with Christian prayer and the Holy Bible. It is an error for a court to say George Washington and our Founding Fathers' doings are unconstitutional. The consequences are divorce is up and families, relationships and our nation have declined since then.

1973: God Disobeyed by Abortion

Ignoring God and our history, a court decided to say abortion "was legal". But God says abortion is murder and is breaking the Ten Commandments. Since this court decision, millions of women and men have guilt from shedding innocent blood, affecting them the rest of their lives–unless they receive God's forgiveness through Jesus (1 John 1:9). Norma McCovey the "Roe" in the court case has become a Christian. She protests against this sin. Shouldn't every Christian speak up to bring an end to abortion?

2000's: Governments Reject George Washington and God's Teachings with Homosexual Sin

George Washington, John Adams, John Jay, Thomas Jefferson, the Jamestown Settlers, the Pilgrims and the people we respect made homosexual sin illegal in our nation. They did this based on God's Word. Do you realize that George Washington said he had "abhorrence and detestation" of homosexual sin and that he said to court-martial homosexuals from the military? For someone to try to remove these laws means they oppose God and George Washington. The person doing so also opposes our Christian nation. If one doesn't like God's laws, then they don't like the USA. Are you also aware that Americans recently voted 32 times in a row against the sin of homosexual "marriage"? Think how much this cost. In addition, there are significant health dangers. The government says one in five homosexuals have HIV (CDC). The average homosexual lifespan is 42 years (Cameron). But to manipulate laws, the government has started preventing the people to vote to try to force homosexual sin. Why would government oppose George Washington? Who would unwisely ignore God's warnings that He judges nations? God destroyed Sodom and Gomorrah for homosexual sin (2 Peter 2:6). Ignoring God and not honoring our Founding Fathers brings more curses.

Crying Out to God Brings God's Deliverance

Let's be honest. Disobeying God is not working for the USA. Sin affects our nation's relationship with God. The

71

consequences affect American's finances, national security, relationships and more. It is the wrong direction. So what does God call His people to do when we have curses from sin? He tells us that crying out to Him and national repentance are His proven answers to us that work. Isaiah 22:4, 12 and Joel 1:14 show the concern Christians should have. They say:

...Do not labor to comfort me because of the plundering of the daughter of my people... And in that day the Lord GOD of hosts called for weeping and for mourning, for baldness and for girding with sackcloth.

Consecrate a fast, call a sacred assembly; Gather the elders and all the inhabitants of the land into the house of the LORD your God, and cry out to the LORD.

Here is God's hope as we decide our future. Do we want blessings for obeying God or curses for disobeying God? As Christians, let's obey God's Word. Does your church cry out to God about our nation's sins as the Holy Bible says to do? Are you crying out to God yourself for the USA? God tells us that *when we cry out to Him, He hears and delivers us.* Please pause and cry out to God about our sins. God remembered His covenant with Israel when they cried out to Him in Egypt (Exodus 2:23-24). Judges 3:9 also promises:

When the children of Israel cried out to the LORD, the LORD raised up a deliverer for the children of Israel, who delivered them...

A "2 Chronicles 7:14 Prayer Group" is helpful. You can form one at your church, school, work or home. Also, USA Christian Ministries has a nation-wide daily email to sign up for. There are tools for churches and groups at: USAChristianMinistries.com. Then, after we cry out to God, God says to call for and organize national repentance.

7

How to Answer God's Call for National Repentance

Father,

Search the USA and know our hearts and see if there is any wicked way in us, and lead us in the way everlasting (Psalm 139:23-24).

In Jesus' name. Amen.

W ould you like the USA to show that we love God? Do you also want God's prosperity and protection? Abigail Adams, wife of one of our greatest Presidents, John Adams, did. She shared, "Righteousness exalts a nation, but sin is a reproach to any people" (Proverbs 14:34). There is no just cause in disobeying God. Are you willing to obey God? That is the first step. Let's look at our nation's sins to know how our nation can repent. Jesus explains the seriousness of sin. He says, "If your foot causes you to sin, cut it off". This means to remove our nation from sin and temptation, not to cut off our foot (Mark 9:45).

The Difference Between the Holy and the Unholy

Two questions to help us know what to repent of are: What are the holy ways of the USA? And what are the unholy ways? Daily reading our Bibles shows us the difference. Here is a danger to avoid. Ezekiel 22:26 says:

Her priests have violated My law and profaned My holy things; they have not distinguished between the holy and unholy, nor have they made known the difference between the unclean and the clean...

As you look at our sins, will you prayerfully consider what God is saying? You are going to have to make a decision. Are you on God's side or sin's side? If you want God's blessings, you must ask honest questions, like: Do the people I vote for submit to God and make Christian laws like our Founding Fathers? Does today's government resist the devil? Do I submit to God and resist the devil, as God says to do? If not, will you agree to start now? The key to living holy is to make the decision to live for God. James 4:7 says:

Therefore submit to God. Resist the devil and he will flee from you.

The Sins of the USA

The USA's sins include:

- **A lukewarm church and efforts to break covenant**
- **The 1947 lie of "separation of church and state"**
- **Not raising children in the Lord**
- **Allowing 53+ million abortions**
- **Not honoring our father and mother**
- **Condoning sexual and homosexual sin**
- **Serving money (mammon)**
- **Voting for ungodly people**
- **Putting trust in something other than God**
- **Not seeking God's counsel**

- **Unbelief that God will save our Christian nation**
- **Being divided instead of keeping the unity of the Spirit**
- **Allowing foreign gods**
- **Selfish individualism and other sin...**

God is a covenant God. He is holy. He wants strong families and a strong Christian nation. He wants to help those lost in sin. That is why He calls for repentance (Acts 20:21).

God's View of a Lukewarm Church and Efforts to Break Covenant

What are Christians doing if we let someone remove the Holy Bible or Ten Commandments from schools or courts? God has been our nation's foundation since day one. What if we listen to someone trying to take the USA away from being a Christian nation? God sees these acts as breaking covenant. The Holy Bible is God's Testament and the Ten Commandments are called "the tablets of the covenant" (Heb. 9:4). God warns that a Christian not caring about Him and our Christian nation is lukewarm. Are you hot or lukewarm? Jeremiah shows that Israel went into captivity for breaking covenant. And in Revelation 3:16 God says He spews the lukewarm out of His mouth. So speak up if someone lies and says God is unconstitutional. It is their ungodly efforts that are unconstitutional. Jeremiah 22:8-9 gives us God's warning:

> **And many nations will pass by this city; and everyone will say to his neighbor, "Why has the LORD done so to this great city?" Then they will answer, "Because they have forsaken the covenant of the LORD their God, and worshiped other gods and served them."**

75

God's View of the
1947 Lie of "Separation of Church and State"

If you were excluded someplace what would you think of those excluding you? So how do you think God feels about a 1947 court deciding against USA history that the government should be separate from God? God sees excluding Him as breaking covenant. We will expose the error of this in detail later, but for now 2 Chronicles 15:2 shows the danger. It says:

The LORD is with you while you are with Him.

God's View of Not Raising Children in the Lord

Here is hope for parents. God gives control of children to the family. He expects each family and the USA to follow Him, starting with the men as leaders. Ephesians 6:4 says:

...Fathers, do not provoke your children to wrath, but bring them up in the training and admonition of the Lord.

What is the best selling book of all time? It is the Holy Bible. God's Word is also the main source our Founding Fathers used, the first book in schools, the first book printed and the only book of God's infallible Word. *Shouldn't children know God, read the best selling book and read what our Founding Fathers founded the USA on?* Imagine how strong the character of our nation will be with our children raised "in the training and admonition of the Lord". Why would God's people want to be like inferior nations that disobey God? Our Founding Fathers' gave us a nation to take care of that had a father's responsibility to raise Christian children and schools teaching the Holy Bible and Christian prayer. So today let's each ask God: "Help us have Your best plans for our children."

76

Whoever doesn't train their children to know God disobeys God. The Ephesians 6:4 verse we read says there are consequences. God's judgment can come in many ways, such as children not honoring their parents, including in old age, or some children rejecting Christ and ending up in hell. It is unwise for your children to gain the world and lose their soul (Matthew 16:26). In comparison, have you seen how wholesome typical Christian homeschool and Christian private school students are? If public schools won't obey God, should the Christian majority support them? God has the best plans for our children. That is why our foremost schoolmaster and author of the Webster's dictionary, Noah Webster, says:

Education is useless without the Bible.

[T]he Christian religion is the most important and one of the first things in which all children, under a free government ought to be instructed.

God's View of Allowing 53+ Million Abortions

To help us live for God, we have a conscience to convict us of sin. That is why there is guilt and suffering after an abortion. Abortion is breaking God's law. Our conscience warns this is wrong. God says abortion is the murder of a human being. Can you see that it is breaking covenant when the USA promotes abortion and uses our citizen's money against our consciences to murder children? God made us to be fathers and mothers. By Christians breaking covenant by not ending government abortion, we bring God's judgment on our nation. Exodus 20:13 says:

Thou shalt not kill. (KJV)

What happens after an abortion? Unless the father and mother cry out for forgiveness through Jesus' blood, then God hears the baby's blood crying out. Genesis 4:10 shows:

What have you done? The voice of your brother's blood cries out to Me from the ground.

Imagine an estimated 53+ million aborted persons' blood crying out to God in the USA. These are Americans that God tells us He knew in the womb (Psalm 139:13-16). This breaking of covenant alone is reason enough for God to allow the USA to be destroyed. However, it is encouraging that more of the USA thinks differently and identifies ourselves as a pro-life nation. In fact, 71% oppose government funded abortions (Zogby, 2008). More Americans are pro-life than not (Gallup 2009 & 2010). Why would our government money be used for sin? God says that abortion is one reason why our nation has been weakened economically and militarily. So what can we do for all Federal, State and Local Governments to repent? We are to join together as Christians and require that abortion be ended in the USA. Don't you want God's love and blessings instead? Let's thank God for the faithful pro-life workers seeking to end this sin.

What About Forgiveness?

Can the father and mother who committed an abortion be forgiven? Can the guilt go away? Yes. Can the abortionist and the staff be forgiven? What about those who made the abortion "laws" and ignored God? What about you and me for our money being used to break God's laws? The answer to each of these questions is yes. *Our Father runs to embrace every American returning to Him,* as in the returning prodigal son. Read Luke 15 to see God's love. 1 John 1:7 and 9 give the extraordinary promise of Jesus forgiving our sins. God says:

The blood of Jesus Christ His Son cleanses us from all sin... If we confess our sins, He is faithful and just to forgive us our sins and to cleanse us from all unrighteousness.

The good news is all sins are cleansed by the blood of Jesus. Have you received God's forgiveness by confessing your sins to God? Do you ask God to help you desire purity and to "turn the hearts of the fathers to the children, and the hearts of the children to their fathers" (Malachi 4:6)? *You can be right with God, forgiven, cleansed and have His peace through Jesus today, no matter what your sin.* God offers each of us a new life when we ask Him. 1 Corinthians 6:11 assures:

And such were some of you. But you were washed, but you were sanctified, but you were justified in the name of the Lord Jesus and by the Spirit of our God.

God's View of Not Honoring Our Father and Mother

Would you like more blessings? God says to honor our father and mother. This also means to take care of your parents by repaying them when they are older (1 Tim. 5:4, 8). So non-Christian "death panels" of "government healthcare" are not God's way. Why? Jesus said, "The thief does not come except to steal, and to kill, and to destroy" (John 10:10). As Christians we are to love our parents. Deut. 5:16 says:

Honor your father and your mother, as the LORD your God has commanded you, that your days may be long, and that it may be well with you...

God's View of Condoning Sexual and Homosexual Sin

Are you encouraged that God wants to dwell with us? God didn't create people for sexual immorality, but for Himself. He wants His Holy Spirit in us. 1 Cor. 6:13 teaches:

79

Now the body is not for sexual immorality but for the Lord, and the Lord for the body.

God created male and female. He shows us that there is a difference between the holy ways of one man and one woman lifelong marriage and the unholy ways of fornication, adultery and homosexual sin. God says that when people commit sexual immorality, they "defile My holy name" and a nation doing so is "defiled" (Amos 2:7, Lev. 18:24). Importantly, He also shows us that every sin a person "does is outside the body, but he who commits sexual immorality sins against his own body" (1 Cor. 6:18). God calls for abstinence before marriage. 1 Cor. 6:9-10 says that the sexually immoral will not go to heaven, unless they repent. Anyone can repent. God says:

Do not be deceived. Neither fornicators... nor adulterers, nor homosexuals, nor sodomites... will inherit the kingdom of God.

All sexual sin is forgiven by Jesus' sacrifice. In the next chapter we share more about God's forgiveness. Let's now look at homosexual sin, to see what God says and to help the USA follow God. Leviticus 18:22 and Deuteronomy 22:5 say:

You shall not lie with a male as with a woman. It is an abomination.

A woman shall not wear anything that pertains to a man, nor shall a man put on a woman's garment, for all who do so are an abomination to the LORD your God.

Now that you are aware of what God says, do you see that a Christian can't support abominations before God? Do you realize that homosexual "marriage" is rejecting what God says? If you are concerned about the consequences of sin,

God tells us to call for repentance and forgiveness. The first mention of sodomy is seen in Genesis 13:13 and later 2 Peter 2:6, Jude 7 and Leviticus 18:25 warn about judgment. They say:

But the men of Sodom were exceedingly wicked and sinful against the LORD.

[God] turning the cities of Sodom and Gomorrah into ashes, condemned them to destruction, making them an example to those who afterward would live ungodly...

...as Sodom and Gomorrah, and the cities around them in a similar manner to these, having given themselves over to sexual immorality and gone after strange flesh, are set forth as an example, suffering the vengeance of eternal fire.

For the land is defiled; therefore I visit the punishment of its iniquity upon it, and the land vomits out its inhabitants.

No one wants the USA judged. God and history show us that God destroys homosexual societies. Kings Asa, Jehoshaphat and Josiah removed homosexual sin from Judah (1 Kings 15:11-12, 1 Kings 22:46, 2 Kings 23:7). 1 Kings 15:11-12 shows King Asa's love for God. It reads:

And Asa did that which was right in the eyes of the LORD, as did David his father. And he took away the sodomites out of the land...

Why does God tell us all this? In Romans 1:22-31 God warns that He gives the unrepentant over to a debased mind. This should be a strong warning that we obey God. He says:

Professing to be wise, they became fools... Therefore God also gave them up to uncleanness, in the lusts of their hearts, to dishonor their bodies

among themselves, who exchanged the truth of God for the lie...

For this reason God gave them up to vile passions. For even their women exchanged the natural use for what is against nature. Likewise also the men, leaving the natural use of the woman, burned in their lust for one another, men with men committing what is shameful, and receiving in themselves the penalty of their error which was due. And even as they did not like to retain God in their knowledge, God gave them over to a debased mind, to do those things which are not fitting; being filled with all unrighteousness, sexual immorality, wickedness... haters of God... who, knowing the righteous judgment of God, that those who practice such things are deserving of death [by God], not only do the same but also approve of those who practice them.

Be careful you are not deceived. Some are lying about what our Founding Fathers believed on sexual sin. The truth is answered with this question: *Who made the laws making homosexual sin illegal in the USA?* Our Founding Fathers, George Washington, John Adams, Thomas Jefferson... made homosexual sin illegal in all thirteen colonies, followed by all fifty states. Why? They obeyed God. They were modest and preferred not to say the word "sodomy" so they called the sin "a crime not fit to be named". George Washington removed by court martial homosexuals out of the military to have God's blessing. You have to decide are you on God's side and our Founding Fathers' side or are you on sin's side. You can't support both. Which side are you on? Now, let's look at our Founding Fathers' beliefs:

Our Founding Fathers Opposed Homosexual Sin

- George Washington -
Court Martialed Homosexuals / Forbid Sin in the Military
...the Commander in Chief... with Abhorrence and Detestation of such Infamous Crimes [sodomy]...

- Ninth Law Made in America -
Laws of Virginia 1610
No man shall commit the horrible and detestable sins of sodomy [homosexuality]...

- Thomas Jefferson -
Authored Bill to Castrate Homosexuals
Crimes whose punishment goes to LIMB. 1. Rape 2. Sodomy } Dismemberment.

- Noah Webster -
Sodomy: A crime against nature. *1828 Dictionary*

- 1833 Encyclopedia Britannica -
The nameless crime, which was the disgrace of Greek and Roman civilization...

- All 13 Colonies & All 50 States Outlawed Homosexual Sin -
New York's Law
That if any man shall lie with mankind as he lieth with womankind, both of them have committed abomination...

Can you see that trying to "change" things in the USA rejects our Founding Fathers? You either have Christianity and the real USA or you have the world and sin. God's purpose for men is to love their wife and to train children in Christ (Ephesians 5:22-6:4). God says, "The fear of the LORD is to hate evil" (Proverbs 8:13). You have to make a

83

decision today. Will you serve God or sin (John 14:21, Psalm 33:12…)? Are you on God's side? God calls those rejecting Him "haters of God" (Romans 1:30). While some early colonial laws had significant penalties for some sins as an effort to keep families strong, they stopped the death penalty. For us today, remember Jesus came to call sinners to repentance. *Jesus simply says, "repent" to sinners. Jesus gave remarkable compassion to the woman caught in adultery. He forgave her, saying, "go, and sin no more" (John 8:11).* Remember God's forgiveness in 1 Corinthians 6:9-11:

> **Do you not know that the unrighteous will not inherit the kingdom of God? Do not be deceived. Neither fornicators… nor adulterers, nor homosexuals, nor sodomites… And such were some of you. But you were washed, but you were sanctified, but you were justified in the name of the Lord Jesus and by the Spirit of our God.**

God's View of Serving Money and the Economy

While God gives blessings to those who love Him, it is also a sin to seek the blessings but not love God. This includes politics. Some say the economy is the most important issue, but Jesus says the Greatest Commandments are most important. He says to "seek first the Kingdom of God and His righteousness" then the blessings of prosperity will be added to us (Matthew 6:33, Deut. 28). Also, do you know that idolatry is covetousness? If the government has a program desiring someone else's wealth for you, that is coveting. When people—whether rich or poor—desire what other people have it is coveting. This results in curses not blessings. God says to share money out of a heart of charity. Let's look to God as our provider not other people. In Matthew 6:24 Jesus says:

No one can serve two masters; for either he will hate the one and love the other, or else he will be loyal to the one and despise the other. You cannot serve God and mammon [riches opposed to God].

While God's people like Abraham and Job had riches, they didn't serve money. They served God who prospered them. They didn't covet other people's items. They loved God and obeyed His commands. As a nation, let's make God our focus. Everyone able is to work for their own needs (Col. 3:5).

Jesus Says: Seek First God Not the Economy

God Says: Love God

Focus: Obey God (Holiness)

Keep Covenant
1. Include the LORD in Families and Government
2. Put Back the Holy Bible and Christian Prayer in Schools
3. Pro-life (End Abortion) and Honor Father & Mother
4. Sexual Purity 1 Man + 1 Woman Marriage
5. Serve Only the LORD
6. Vote for God-fearing People
7. Unity of the Spirit
8. Believe God Will Help
9. Each Person Works and Trusts in God...

Then God Adds Blessings

Result: All These Things Added

God's Blessings...

Loving God Adds Blessings

- Economic Prosperity
- Low Taxes / No Debt
- National Security No Terrorism in USA
- Peace
- Freedom

#1: Seek First The Kingdom of God And His Righteousness...

Covenant Christian Nation

Wrong Priority It is Wrong to Seek God's Blessings But Not God

Love God Love One Another

Read: Matthew 6:33, Deuteronomy 28, Leviticus 26, 2 Corinthians 3:17 Psalm 33:12 and 2 Chronicles 15

85

God's View of Voting for Ungodly People

What happens if a Christian votes for those disobeying God? What are the consequences? 2 Chronicles 19:2 gives God's warning. We see that king Jehoshaphat had helped king Ahab, who God says was wicked. In response, God warns:

Should you help the wicked and love [have human love for] those who hate the LORD? Therefore the wrath of the LORD is upon you.

Instead of bringing God's blessing, helping the ungodly brings God's wrath. Jehoshaphat again helped the ungodly and his work was ruined. 2 Chronicles 20:35-37 shows:

Jehoshaphat king of Judah allied himself with Ahaziah king of Israel, who acted very wickedly... Because you have allied yourself with Ahaziah, the LORD has destroyed your works.

Psalm 1:1 says the USA will have blessings if we don't walk in the counsel of ungodly politicians. It says:

Blessed is the man who walks not in the counsel of the ungodly, nor stands in the path of sinners, nor sits in the seat of the scornful;

God's blessings come when we avoid what is not of God. This includes ungodly movies, people... Romans 16:17, Titus 3:10-11 and 1 Corinthians 5:13 say:

Now I urge you, brethren, note [mark] those who cause divisions and offenses, contrary to the doctrine which you learned, and avoid them.

Reject a divisive man after the first and second admonition, knowing that such a person is warped and sinning, being self-condemned.

...put away (separate) from yourselves the evil person.

86

Do you know that God tells us to mark, reject and to put away (separate from) the person who tries to bring the USA from being a Christian nation? To draw a nation away from God is the worse sin someone can commit against a nation (Deuteronomy 13, 2 Chronicles 15:13). For us today God says to reject the person unless they repent. Jesus died to forgive sins, but the non-repentant sinner God doesn't accept. Psalm 11:5 and 40:4 say:

> **The LORD tests the righteous, but the wicked and the one who loves violence His soul hates...**
>
> **Blessed is that man who makes the LORD his trust, and does not respect the proud, nor such as turn aside to lies.**

God's View of Putting Trust in Something Other than God

Are you encouraged that God has better plans for the USA than sin? Our national motto is: In God we trust. But if we rely on something other than God, it can be used to harm the USA. This includes trusting in political parties, government, news stations and others instead of God. Judah trusted in Egypt to save them from the sword of Babylon. As a result, the sword overtook them in Egypt. Jeremiah 42:13-16 says:

> **But if you say... "we will go to the land of Egypt where we shall see no war, nor hear the sound of the trumpet, nor be hungry for bread, and there we will dwell" – Then hear now the word of the LORD... "If you wholly set your faces to enter Egypt, and go to dwell there, then it shall be that the sword which you feared shall overtake you there in the land of Egypt; the famine of which you were afraid shall follow close after you..."**

87

God's View of Not Seeking His Counsel

Jesus says to abide in Him. In John 15:5 He said:

I am the vine, you are the branches. He who abides in Me, and I in him, bears much fruit; for without Me you can do nothing.

More good news is that we are created to continually seek God's counsel for the USA. By seeking God's counsel, our nation won't be deceived. In Matthew 4:4 Jesus explains:

Man shall not live by bread alone, but by every word that proceeds from the mouth of God.

The Greek word for "word" in this verse is *rhema*, which means God's revealed word. As Israel was led by the cloud by day and the fire by night, the USA is to seek God.

God's View of Unbelief that He Will Save Our Christian Nation

Are you ready for God's miraculous help? This requires faith in God. Israel "could not enter in because of unbelief" (Heb. 3:19). Some people doubt. But God expects us to have faith He will help the USA. Hebrews 11:6 and Zeph. 1:12 say:

But without faith it is impossible to please Him, for he who comes to God must believe that He is, and that He is a rewarder of those who diligently seek Him.

I will search... the men who are settled in complacency, who say in their heart, 'The LORD will not do good, nor will He do evil.'

God's View of Allowing Foreign Gods

The LORD alone is God. He made the heavens and the earth (Genesis 1:1). Deuteronomy 6:14-15 say:

You shall not go after other gods, the gods of the peoples who are all around you (for the LORD your God is a jealous God among you)...

In Romans 11:22, we learn that there is goodness for those who obey God and severity for those who disobey Him. If the USA has foreign gods, God says He will not deliver the USA from our enemies. A foreign god is any other god than the LORD (Father, Son and Holy Spirit). Judges 10:13-14 read:

Yet you have forsaken Me and served other gods. Therefore I will deliver you no more...

It is encouraging that God blesses the people that put away foreign gods. God is merciful when He sees repentance. Israel repented in Judges 10:5-16 by saying to the LORD:

We have sinned... So they put away the foreign gods from among them and served the LORD...

God's View of Being Divided

We have two more sins to look at. Now think of God's love. God cares for us perfectly. That is why He calls for the unity of the Spirit (Ephesians 4:3). Remember God doesn't acknowledge "right," "left," "diversity," or anything but Himself (Joshua 5:13-14). Therefore if Christians are divided, then the USA will fall. But let's unite in Christ. Diversity, or to mix with those not in Christ, can mean to reach the lowest common denominator of Christians and non-Christians. Diversity is often used to dilute the Christian majority mixing light and darkness. It is often unBiblical as one common use of diversity includes sexual sin (Gal. 5:9). The Christian majority would be better by not using "diversity" (Deut. 22:9 KJV, Heb. 13:9 KJV). It is helpful to use Biblical words instead for our common language. Do you remember Jesus' warning in Matthew 12:25? He says:

89

[Every] house divided against itself will not stand...

God's View of Selfish Individualism

As Christians we love one another. We are part of Christ's body. Imagine if everyone in a family only promoted their own selfish individualism, then the family would be less than it could be. This is why we are to live as a Christian family in the USA. That is how God sees us. Ephesians 4:15-16 reads:

...the head–Christ–from whom the whole body, joined and knit together by what every joint supplies, according to the effective working by which every part does its share, causes growth of the body for the edifying of itself in love.

Join in National Repentance

God loves us. He has the best plans for the USA. That is why He wants the heart of every American. Will you give your heart to God? There are two steps for national repentance. As the first step, will you agree with God that the USA is to repent of the sins in this chapter? Just tell God that you agree with Him. He sees everyone agreeing with Him. Then as a second step, work and actively call for national repentance so our nation can love God and one another.

Two Steps of National Repentance

1. **Agree with God the USA's Sins Are to End**
2. **Repent as a Nation**

God loves us. You can log your decision of agreement online at USAChristianMinistries.com. 2 Chron. 7:14 assures:

If My people... will turn from their wicked ways, then I will hear from heaven, and will forgive their sin and heal their land.

90

8

God's Mercy:
Jesus' Sacrifice Forgives the USA

Father,

We receive forgiveness for our nation's sins by Jesus' blood sacrifice. We hope in Your mercy for the USA.

In Jesus' Name.

While God loves us as our Father, the USA's sins against Him must be forgiven. Atonement is the only way that the consequences from disobeying God can be stopped. But how can the nation's sins be forgiven? Let's look at God's answer to forgive our sin.

God Wants to Give Mercy to Our Nation

Do you know God's mercy? The Holy Bible teaches that God wants to show mercy for repentance rather than judgment for sin. We see that after David made atonement for Israel's sin, "the LORD heeded the prayers for the land, and the plague was withdrawn" (2 Samuel 24:25). The key to forgiveness is to know that God is merciful and gracious. Exodus 34:6 reveals this secret as God passed before Moses. It is written:

And the LORD passed before him and proclaimed, "The LORD, the LORD God, merciful

and gracious, longsuffering, and abounding in goodness and truth…"

It Pleased God to Bruise Jesus

While God loves Americans and desires to show mercy, if there is no atonement for our sins then there is only judgment for breaking God's laws. Even an earthly parent can desire to do many good things for their child, but if the child disobeys then the parent disciplines and takes things away from the child. However, *in mercy, Jesus bore our sins. He suffered for us. God put His wrath for our sins on Jesus.* The atonement for our Christian nation's sin is through Jesus. This is a covenant promise. Isaiah 53:10-11 says:

> **Yet it pleased the LORD to bruise Him [Jesus]; He has put Him to grief. When You make His soul an offering for sin… He shall see the labor of His soul, and be satisfied. By His knowledge My righteous Servant shall justify many, for He shall bear their iniquities.**

The Cross Says the USA is Forgiven

Here is God's mercy. Instead of paying for our sins in God's judgment, we can receive God's forgiveness through Jesus Christ. Jesus bore our sins on the Cross. By faith in Jesus, the USA is also forgiven. While each person needs to ask God to forgive them personally, the church by covenant accepts God's forgiveness of the USA. You can do this now. *Will you agree that Jesus' blood forgives our nation's sins?* We are in covenant. This is our promise. By repenting from our sins, we glorify God. When David cried out to God for mercy, the Lord in His mercy ended the plague we mentioned earlier. This shows that the church in our Christian nation is also to ask God for mercy. In 2 Samuel 24:14, David said:

Please let us fall into the hand of the LORD, for His mercies are great...

Only Jesus' Blood Sacrifice Forgives the USA

Think about Jesus' perfect work on the Cross to forgive your sin. Likewise, God says there is nothing that can forgive our nation's sin–except the blood of Jesus. 1 John 1:7 assures:

... the blood of Jesus Christ His Son cleanses us from all sin.

God wants to forgive our nation. Joel 2:12-13 promises:

Turn to Me with all your heart, with fasting, with weeping, and with mourning. So rend your heart [tear apart the evil from our hearts in repentance], and not your garments; Return to the LORD your God, for He is gracious and merciful,

93

slow to anger, and of great kindness; And He relents from doing harm.

Will You Accept God's Forgiveness for the USA?

God gives forgiveness by faith in Jesus Christ. Will you humble yourself before God now and receive God's forgiveness for our nation's sins by Jesus' sacrifice on the cross? Pastors, will you lead your church in agreeing that Jesus' blood forgives the USA? Join in prayer:

Father,

Your mercy endures forever. We are a covenant Christian nation. The blood of Jesus Christ Your Son cleanses the USA from all sin. (2 Chronicles 20:21, Psalm 147:11, 1 John 1:7)

We ask You to circumcise the USA's hearts to love righteousness and not wickedness, including to:

- **Welcome You and include You in government,**
- **Train our children in You in school with the Holy Bible and Christian prayer,**
- **Be sexually pure and to love the unborn,**
- **Honor our father and mother,**
- **Obey You with one man and one woman lifetime marriage,**
- **Worship only You – removing foreign gods,**
- **Serve You not money, and**
- **Obey You in all things.** (1 John 1:7-9)

In Jesus' name. Amen.

9

God's Solution:
Unite the USA in Christ

Father,

We humble ourselves as Christians and unite in

Christ.

In Jesus' name. Amen.

How can we keep our nation strong? Let's look at our Founding Fathers to see what they did. When they first prayed in Congress in 1774, they united in Christ. As Christians of different denominations, they agreed on the major doctrines to work together. This is how the revolution was won. It is also how we are to work together in Christ.

The Unity of the Spirit

As God's people and as the majority of the USA, Christians are God's way of unifying our nation. Ephesians 4:3 and Psalm 133:1 say:

...Endeavoring to keep the unity of the Spirit in the bond of peace.

...How good and how pleasant it is for brethren to dwell together in unity!

Notice the first verse says, "The unity of the Spirit". God doesn't mean the "unity of man". The "unity of man" would result in a compromise which is not of God. *The Bible says, "The unity of the Spirit".* This means to be united in the Spirit of God, which is being united in God's Word. There are two ways for Christians to have unity. They are for Christians to:

1. **Unite in the Holy Spirit,** and

2. **Unite in the Holy Bible.**

These two agree and never contradict each other. For example, it would be a contradiction for someone to say, "The Holy Spirit is leading me to live with someone before marriage". The reason is because that is not the Holy Spirit for the Bible says, "Do not be deceived. Neither fornicators... nor adulterers... nor homosexuals... will inherit the Kingdom of God". God would not have you act against His Word (1 Corinthians 6:9-10).

God doesn't tell Christians to unite "as Christians". Instead, He tells Christians to unite in Christ. *This means to unite in God.* Otherwise, we would unite in our own ideas. We would do what each person thinks is right, not what God says is right. That kind of "unity" is not from God. It is the unity of man. Instead, we are to yield to God. Many things we hear are not from God. As we saw, the term "diversity" is not a Christian term. When you hear a politician say, "let's work for all Americans" or "diversity" they often mean to water-down the Christian majority. To be unequally yoked is not God's best plans for the USA. God wants all people to follow Him. Do you see this snare keeps people from uniting in Christ as our Founding Fathers said? It weakens the USA.

God's Plan Versus Satan's Plan

God's Plan: Unite the USA in Christ™

"I am the vine, you are the branches. He who abides in Me, and I in him, bears much fruit." Jesus Christ (John 15:5)

God's Protection

Prosperity

Brotherly Love

Live for God

✠ Covenant Christian Nation

A Family

Follow Christ

Strong Families

Christian Laws (Holy Bible)

Blessed Nation

Covenant Nation

Freedom

Deuteronomy 28 Blessings

Satan's Plan: Divide the USA

"Without Me you can do nothing" Jesus Christ (John 15:5)

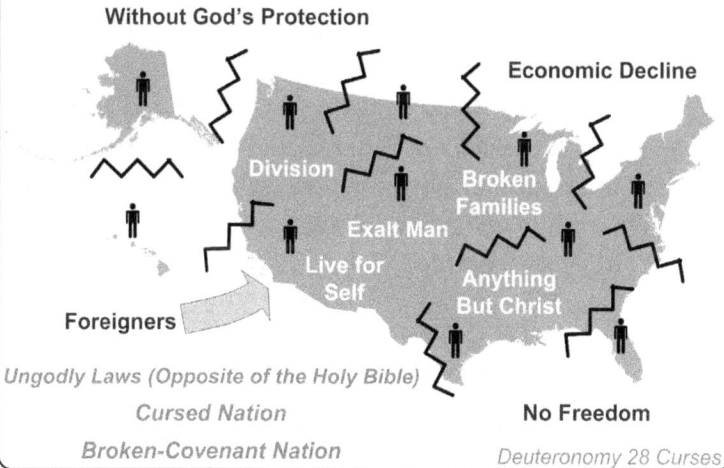

Without God's Protection

Economic Decline

Division

Broken Families

Exalt Man

Live for Self

Anything But Christ

Foreigners

Ungodly Laws (Opposite of the Holy Bible)

Cursed Nation

Broken-Covenant Nation

No Freedom

Deuteronomy 28 Curses

97

More importantly, God has one message and that is "unite in Me," not unite in diversity. Our life is in Christ. How could God's people unite with people who practice sin, follow foreign gods or try to remove God from things? God forbids this (Exodus 23:33-34, 1 Corinthians 6:9-10). To follow Jesus on the straight and narrow path means not to be led astray with a different gospel (Galatians 1:6).

The USA is Blessed by Uniting in Christ

Have you been thinking, "What can I do to unite my family, community, state and our nation in Christ?" A good place to start is to fill your family and the USA with God's Word. You can:

- Add Bibles verses to articles, speeches, videos, blogs, text messages, lunch boxes, radio shows, advertising, billboards and other places (John 15:7),
- Boldly speak God's word (Acts 4:29),
- Pastors: Teach the difference between what is holy and what is unholy / clean and unclean (Ezekiel 22:26),
- Political Groups and the Tea Party: Be called "Christians" instead of "conservatives" (Romans 1:16)
- Government Servants: Make God's laws our laws–as our Founding Fathers said to do (Psalm 33:12),
- Schools, Teachers & Parents: Undo ungodly laws. Share God's truth and pray for your school or homeschool– Train children in the training and admonition of the Lord (Ephesians 6:4), and
- Judges: Follow God's laws (Rev. 20:12, Psalm 2:10-12).

Christians are Family

God calls Christians His family. This means that every Christian in the USA is God's family. Ephesians 3:15 shares:

...I bow my knees unto the Father of our Lord Jesus Christ, of whom the whole family in heaven and earth is named...

As God's family, let's encourage one another with God's love and hope. Do you look at the USA as a Christian family? By uniting in Christ, we:

- Declare: The LORD is the God of the USA and we are His people (Psalm 33:12, 2 Corinthians 6:16),
- Keep the unity of the Spirit in the bond of peace (Ephesians 4:3),
- Seek God's counsel for our nation (Joshua 9:14),
- Love one another as Jesus loved us (John13:34),
- Care for one another (1 Corinthians 12:25),
- Forgive one another (Ephesians 4:32), and
- Pray for one another (James 5:16).

What Every Christian Agrees On

Every Christian should agree on the following:

God the Father, God the Son and God the Holy Spirit
God eternally exists in three Persons as God the Father, God the Son and God the Holy Spirit. (2 Corinthians 13:14)

Jesus Christ is Lord and Savior
Jesus Christ is the head of the church. Each Christian is to call on Jesus as Lord and Savior. We are to come out of the world, crucify our flesh (sinful nature) and follow Jesus. (Matt. 16:24)

The Holy Bible is God's Word
The Holy Bible is the infallible Word of God, the authority on what God says. It is how He wants us to live. (2 Tim. 3:16-17)

Each Person Will Perish Without Jesus Christ
All have sinned, fall short of the glory of God and therefore face the judgment of God for their sin. Each person individually is to call on Jesus Christ to be saved. Jesus lived a perfect sinless life. He is the Lamb of God who takes away the sin of the world. He died and rose from the dead. The blood of Jesus shed on the cross cleanses us from all sin. (Romans 3:23, Romans 6:23, John 1:29, John 3:16, Acts 4:12, Ephesians 2:8-9, 1 John 1:7)

We Are to Live the Greatest Commandments
The First Commandment is to "love the Lord your God with all your heart, with all your soul, with all your mind, and with all your strength." In John 13:34 Jesus makes the Second Commandment new saying, "love one another; as I have loved you, that you also love one another". This is how to "love your neighbor as yourself." We are to follow Jesus and seek and do the Father's will. (Mark 12:30, John 13:34, Matt.7:21)

Christians Are to Live Holy and Abundant Lives
God gives us the Holy Spirit who helps us live a holy and abundant life–glorifying God. (Galatians 5:22-23, 1 Peter 1:14-16, Romans 8:14, 1 Cor. 12, 2 Cor. 6:17, John 10:10)

Christians are to be like Jesus, rejecting anything that contradicts His Word, including sin, the devil and the world. As Christians, let's work together in Christ since every Christian can agree on these guidelines. However, if someone denies these things, then God says to avoid that person (Romans 16:17, Galatians 1:8-9).

If you haven't done so already, there are three decisions to make to know God personally: 1) Call on the Lord Jesus Christ to save you from your sins (see Prayer of Salvation section); 2) Claim Jesus Christ to be Lord of your life; and 3) Daily pray and read one or more chapters of the Holy Bible.

10

Remove the Lie of
"Separation of Church and State"

Father,

*Like our Founding Fathers, we include You in
every part of our government. We ask You to fill
our nation with Yourself. In Jesus' Name. Amen.*

It is a righteous cause to work for Christian freedom and to repent of national sin. Will you welcome God to every part of the USA including all of government? A priority for pastors, Christians and the government is to remove the lie of "separation of church and state". The word lie is used because this myth is:

1. Not What our Founding Fathers Practiced or Intended,
2. Not Constitutional,
3. Not Historical, and
4. Sin Against God.

Four Truths to Remove "Separation of Church and State"

Truth 1: The Founding Fathers Combined Christianity and the Government

Our Founding Fathers' practice was to keep the state out of the Christian church, not the church out of the state. This is why they came to the USA. They made a "Covenant of

Dedication [to] remain to all generations, as long as this earth remains". The point has been made that our Founding Fathers included God in all parts of government and life. They prayed publicly in Jesus' name, had Christian Church services in the USA Capital, taught the Gospel of Jesus Christ in schools and much more. They welcomed God to fill all things–including all the government. This is the intent of the USA. Our nation's history shows this truth. Jesus Christ and our government are combined. Will you come into agreement with God and include Him in all things in the USA?

With thanksgiving and praise our Founding Fathers declared the Lord is the God of the USA and we are His people. James Madison who wrote the Constitution declared that he saw the finished Constitution as a product of "the finger of that Almighty Hand which has been so frequently and signally extended to our relief in the critical stages of the Revolution". The First Amendment was written to give Christian freedom.

President Lincoln Taking Presidential Oath on the Holy Bible

102

Our covenant with the one true God provides the foundation of our laws and it is why the USA has been blessed above all nations. As we saw earlier, hundreds of years after the Jamestown settlers, and over one hundred years after the signing of the First Amendment, the 1892 Supreme Court said:

...this is a Christian nation.

All Government Has Combined Christianity in Government

It is hypocrisy to talk about "separation of church and state" because all government has included God, including:

- *Jamestown Settlers, Pilgrims...*
- *Signers of the Declaration of Independence*
- *Congress and Continental Congress*
- *George Washington, John Adams, John Hancock...*
- *Thomas Jefferson, James Madison, Abraham Lincoln...*
- *The Constitution*
- *Every President – Takes their oath on the Holy Bible*
- *Supreme Court and Courts*
- *USA Capital – Including Christian church in the Capital*
- *Delaware, Maryland, California... All Fifty States*
- *Schools, Military and Currency*
- *Washington Monument, Lincoln & Jefferson Memorials...*
- *Federal Holidays: Christmas and Thanksgiving*

Truth 2: The Constitution Combines Christianity and Government
The Constitution contains *"the year of our Lord"*. This means the Constitution is a Christian document acknowledging Jesus Christ as Lord of the USA. However, the term "separation of church and state" is not found anywhere in the Constitution. *The Constitution says the opposite of what we are often told.* The Supreme Court referenced the Constitution to say, "this is

a Christian nation" in 1892. If the signers did not want God in the government, they would have removed "the year of our Lord". Instead, Benjamin Franklin *called for prayer* at the Constitutional Convention. Our Founding Fathers on purpose included our Lord Jesus Christ in the Constitution to reaffirm our covenant. Also, Article 1 Section 7 of the Constitution says "Sundays excepted" to honor the Lord. We saw that Justice Storey explained the First Amendment was for Christians. It also says that Congress shall make no law prohibiting the free exercise of [Christian] religion. That is three references to God in the Constitution. Someone may say what about the Establishment Clause? The First Amendment includes what is called the "Establishment Clause". It says that Christian religion is the established religion of the USA:

Congress shall make no law respecting an establishment of [one Christian denomination] religion, or prohibiting the free exercise [of Christian religion] thereof...

In 1799 the Supreme Court of Maryland affirmed:

<u>By our form of government, the Christian religion is the established religion;</u> and all sects and denominations of Christians are placed on the same equal footing.

Christianity is the established religion with no one Christian denomination above another. There is no mention of other "religions" in the Constitution–only Christianity. Does anyone really think that our Christian Founding Fathers would undermine the Christian freedom of the USA that they risked their lives for? And does anyone believe our Founding Fathers would write the First Amendment to limit Christianity and then violate the First Amendment daily afterwards? Of course not! For example, George Washington issued a Thanksgiving

Proclamation to God a week after Congress approved the First Amendment. Our Founding Fathers filled every aspect of government with Christianity. Their concern was to prevent the government from limiting the Gospel of Jesus Christ.

Looking at history, we see the Constitution was ratified in 1788 and the First Amendment was ratified in 1791. We saw how Washington, Adams, Jay, Lincoln... combined Christian churches into the state. Thomas Jefferson was not involved; in the Constitution and was in France when the First Amendment was written. Eleven years later, in a *personal letter* in 1802 Jefferson thought the government shouldn't interfere with the Danbury Baptists by setting up one Christian denomination controlled by the state as Europe had. He said the government couldn't do this because of a "wall of separation," which meant to keep the world (ungodliness) away from God's people. His personal letter was for Christian religious liberty. Did you know that Jefferson combined Christian churches into the "state"? Jefferson and Madison endorsed Christian church in the USA Capital, as well as God. For example, Jefferson mentioned prayer and God in his Danbury Baptist letter and then attended Christian church inside the Capital two days after sending the letter. Jefferson went to Christian church in the Capital ongoing afterwards. He also authorized Christian church services in the War Office and the Treasury building. In 1803, he extended the 1787 Act of Congress to designate government land for promoting Christianity. It reads:

... for the sole use of Christian Indians and the Moravian Brethren Missionaries for the civilizing of the Indians and promoting Christianity.

In 1806 and 1807 Jefferson and the government promoted Christianity to the Wyandotte/Cherokee Indians. Jefferson used "in the year of our Lord Christ" for his presidential signature.

Also, James Wilson who was in the *original Supreme Court*, signed the Declaration of Independence and the Constitution, spoke 168 times at the Constitutional Convention and wrote legal textbooks for American education. He taught the USA that human law must rest its authority on God's law. He wrote:

> **All [laws], however, may be arranged in two different classes, 1) Divine [God]. 2) Human... Human law must rest its authority ultimately upon the authority of that law which is Divine [God].**

Truth 3: The "Separation of Church and State" Lies Are Not Found in USA History

Starting in 1607 Americans used the Ten Commandments to make laws. The Supreme Court/government have said we are a "Christian nation," Christian people," Christian country..." We combine Christian churches and government. Jefferson combined Christian churches and government. The Supreme Court opens with "God save the United States and this honorable court". "Separation of church and state" isn't found in American history until 1947 when an activist court made it up with bad law. The activist court took eight words of Jefferson's *private letter* to falsely make a biased ruling against our nation's history and our Founding Fathers. The court ignored the rest. Justice Black had been active with the Ku Klux Klan and was biased. He also took prayer out of school. This twisting is how the myth came about. Jefferson's "wall of separation" isn't used legally before 1947 except in 1878 for something different. Have you seen the erroneous news and Internet articles of "separation of church and state"?

Truth 4: God Expects His Laws to Be Our Laws

"In the beginning God created the heavens and the earth" (Genesis 1:1). It is our duty to follow Him. If the USA doesn't follow God's laws, then what inferior laws are we following? The question is: Do we love God? In John 14:21, Jesus says:

He who has My commandments and keeps them, it is he who loves Me.

A country rejects God by having the false belief of "separation of church and state" against Christian churches. How many of the USA's broken families and wars are from excluding God and missing His blessings? History also shows that any government that separates itself from God becomes corrupt. Efforts to keep the LORD out of government mean that Satan influences the government, because God would not be welcome. Satan is a living being who leads nations astray. If a nation rejects God, then God will reject that nation (2 Chronicles 15:2). Can you imagine the lawlessness and corruption of such a place? Just think of children without God's hope, or unholy laws being made. Separation of God from the government is what Socialist and Communist countries do. Satan then takes God's freedom and financial blessings away from the people. We need to listen to God's warning and work to remove these lies so the USA can be blessed. If presidents or Congress don't obey God, then vote for better people who will obey God. Your and your family's future depends on the USA including God. Psalm 9:17 shows:

The wicked shall be turned into hell, and all the nations that forget God.

Our Founding Fathers Combined Christian Churches and Government

Look at these twenty-five reasons showing our Founding Fathers combined Christian denominations and the state. We have God's blessings when we welcome God as a nation.

Twenty-Five Reasons Showing the USA
Combines Christian Churches and Government

1. All the USA government has endorsed Christianity.
2. Our Founding Fathers ratified the First Amendment in
   1791 to protect the "liberties of the Gospel" they fought
   for. For example, George Washington in 1795 gave:

   **A proclamation: <u>By the President</u> of the United
   States of America... it is, in an especial manner, <u>our
   duty as people</u>, with devout reverence and affectionate
   gratitude, <u>to acknowledge our many and great
   obligations to Almighty God</u> and to implore Him to
   continue and confirm the blessings we experience.**

3. The Constitution includes Jesus and endorses God. It says,
   "The year of our Lord". To honor the Lord Article 1
   Section 7 includes "except Sundays". The First
   Amendment includes God: "Congress shall make no law...
   prohibiting the free exercise of [Christian religion]".
4. *The Constitution doesn't contain the words, "Separation
   of church and state". It says the opposite, endorsing God.*
5. Supreme Court Justice Joseph Story also explained in
   1833 that *the First Amendment means Christianity only,
   not any other belief.* Justice Story's popular work was
   reprinted 72 years. Madison appointed Story, who wrote:

   **The real object of the [First] Amendment was, not
   to countenance [approve], much less to advance
   Mohammedanism, or Judaism, or infidelity [secular-
   ism], by prostrating Christianity, but to exclude all
   rivalry among Christian sects [denominations]...**

6. *Our national motto is: "In God we trust".* Our currency
   says, "In God we trust". Our national anthem declares,
   "in God is our trust". These government decisions were
   made after the 1802 personal letter of Jefferson.

7. James Wilson, Supreme Court Justice appointed by George Washington and signer of the Constitution, said:
   "Human law must rest its authority ultimately upon the authority of that law which is divine... Far from being rivals or enemies, [Christian] religion and law are twin sisters, friends, and mutual assistants."

8. Jefferson attended Christian church in the USA Capital, where the Marine band led worship. After Jefferson, government continued to endorse Christian churches.

9. As President, Jefferson signed bills that appropriated funds for chaplains in Congress and the military, promoting Christianity to the Indians on government land, and signed, "In the year of our Lord Christ" as President...

10. Jefferson did not write, sign or ratify the Constitution. He was in France when the First Amendment was written. A personal letter by Jefferson wouldn't affect our Constitution. Jefferson includes God in his Danbury Baptists personal letter, writing, "I reciprocate your kind prayers..." How could Jefferson contradict himself? Also, why isn't the 1813 Adams to Jefferson letter used? It says:
    The general Principles, on which the Fathers Achieved Independence, were... the general Principles of Christianity, in which all those sects were united...

11. Thomas Jefferson wrote, "All men are endowed by their Creator" in the Declaration of Independence.

12. The Jefferson Memorial testifies, "God who gave us life gave us liberty. Can the liberties of a nation be secure when we have removed a conviction that these liberties are the gift of God?" Additionally, the government has endorsed God after the 1947 twisting of a personal letter.

13. Jefferson wanted to protect the freedom of Christian churches from a state controlled church. A personal letter of Thomas Jefferson contains "wall of separation," but

Jefferson meant that the government could not breach God's authority with Christian churches.

14. The 1799 Supreme Court of Maryland affirmed that Christianity is the USA's established religion. In 1892 the Supreme Court said, "...this is a Christian nation".

15. In the Gettysburg Address, Abraham Lincoln affirmed, "this nation, under God". This is on the Lincoln Memorial.

16. In 1870, the USA Government made the birth of Christ, Christmas, an official holiday. Thanksgiving to God for His blessings to us is also a government holiday.

17. Our Founding Fathers established our government on Isaiah 33:22, with the three branches of government: "For the LORD is our Judge, the LORD is our Lawgiver, the LORD is our King; He will save us".

18. After Thomas Jefferson, John Quincy Adams our sixth President, said on the Fourth of July 1821 and 1837:

The highest glory of the American Revolution was this: it connected in one indissoluble bond, the principles of civil government with the principles of Christianity... From the day of the Declaration... they [Americans] were bound by the laws of God, which they all, and by the laws of The Gospel, which they nearly all, acknowledged as the rules of their conduct.

Why is it that, next to the birthday of the Savior of the World, your most joyous and most venerated festival returns [4th of July] on this day... Is it not that, in the chain of human events, the birthday of the nation is indissolubly linked with the birthday of the Savior? ... That it laid the cornerstone of human government upon the first precepts of Christianity...

19. Deut. 28 and Lev. 26 show that God blesses the USA for obeying Him and curses the USA for disobeying Him.

20. Jefferson's letter has one reference in court before 1947. It is unrelated. It is an error to twist: "Congress shall make no law respecting an establishment of [one Christian denomination] religion, or prohibiting the free exercise [of Christian religion]" with: "Separation of church and state".

21. Andrew Jackson, our seventh President, assured us, "The Bible is the Rock on which this Republic rests."

22. In 1821 the author of our national anthem, Francis Scott Key, said, "The patriot who feels himself in the service of God... will therefore seek to establish for his country in the eyes of the world, such a character as shall make her not unworthy of the name of a Christian nation..."

23. Noah Webster said, "This is genuine Christianity, and to this we owe our free constitutions of government."

24. Daniel Webster said, "Our fathers were brought hither by their high veneration for the Christian religion... They sought to incorporate its [Christian religion] principles with the elements of their society, and to diffuse its influence through all their institutions, civil, political, or literary."

25. *At the Constitutional Convention in 1787, Benjamin Franklin testified of the need for daily prayer. He said:*

In the beginning of the Contest with G. Britain, when we were sensible of danger we had daily prayer in this room for the divine protection. Our prayers, Sir, were heard, and they were graciously answered... And have we now forgotten that powerful friend?

I have lived, Sir, a long time, and the longer I live, the more convincing proofs I see of this truth - that <u>God governs in the affairs of men. And if a sparrow cannot fall to the ground without his notice, is it probable that an empire can rise without his aid?</u>

We have been assured, Sir, in the sacred writings, that "<u>except the Lord build the House</u> they labour in

vain that build it." I firmly believe this; and I also believe that without his concurring aid we shall succeed in this political building no better than the Builders of Babel: We shall be divided by our little partial local interests... we ourselves shall become a reproach and bye word down to future ages... <u>I therefore beg leave to move, that henceforth prayers imploring the assistance of Heaven, and its blessings on our deliberations, be held in this Assembly every morning before we proceed</u> to business, and that one or more of the [Christian] Clergy of the City be requested to officiate in that service.

Isn't it Treason to Betray Our Founding Fathers?

How many of the USA's problems are because of excluding God? To have God's blessings, Christians are to ask God to the fill every part of the USA. *Our Founding Fathers combined Christian churches and government.* They refused one state church that weakens worship. Furthermore, it was never the intent to not have Christian churches with government. Whoever promotes the lie of "separation of church and state" betrays George Washington, John Adams and God Himself. Because "separation" is sin, how outraged do you think our Founding Fathers would be at the unthankful people saying not to display God's Ten Commandments or a nativity scene, or to pray in Jesus' name? Lowering the USA to the world's ways hurts our nation. Will you help bring back God's blessings? God expects us to reject and quickly remove the lie of "separation of church and state". It is:

1. Not What our Founding Fathers Practiced or Intended,
2. Not Constitutional,
3. Not Historical, and
4. Sin Against God.

11

God's Best Plans Are to Have No King but Jesus

Father,

We declare Jesus Christ is Lord and King of the USA.

In Jesus' name. Amen.

D o you remember God saying that He is the King of the earth and that He reigns over the nations? Psalm 47:7-9 says:

For God is the King of all the earth; Sing praises with understanding. God reigns over the nations; God sits on His holy throne... the shields of the earth belong to God; He is greatly exalted.

The Father has placed all things under Jesus (1 Cor. 15:27-28). Therefore, since our Christian nation is God's by covenant, Americans serve Jesus Christ as King of the USA.

Jesus is King of the USA

To live for Jesus is normal for Americans. When the Governor of Boston reported to King George, he said:

If you ask an American, who is his master? He will tell you he has none, nor any governor but Jesus Christ.

George Washington recognized Jesus Christ as Lord and King. Washington called every American to seek God. Our first president told everyone in our nation to seek God frequently. Here are two examples in 1789 and 1795:

> **By the President of the United States of America. A proclamation... that we may then unite in most humbly offering our prayers and supplications to <u>the great Lord and Ruler of Nations</u>, and beseech Him to pardon our national and other transgressions...**

> **A proclamation: By the President of the United States of America... I, George Washington, President of the United States, do recommend... <u>to all persons whomsoever</u>, within the United States, to set apart and observe Thursday, the nineteenth day of February next [1795], as a day of public thanksgiving and prayer: and on that day <u>to meet together and render their sincere and hearty thanks to the great Ruler of nations</u> for the manifold and signal mercies which distinguish our lot as a nation.**

Do you see that our Founding Fathers answered God's call with joy and gladness of heart? They made Jesus King. Americans testified they had "no King but King Jesus". They obeyed God instead of the "state" when it disobeyed God. We also are to fear God not people. Remember the prophets rebuked "man kings" who disobeyed God.

Think how unwise it would be for a nation not to live under God's dominion. That would be a hopeless life without God's forgiveness, protection and deliverance. Corruption and immorality would ruin families and the government.

Where do God's best plans come from? The answer is God. He asks every American to call upon Him to be King of the USA willingly from our hearts (Isaiah 33:22, Philippians 2:11). This is how we can have God's abundant plans. With Jesus as our King we are in right relationship with God. Here is an important key for you. Will you make Jesus to be Lord and King of your life and the USA? Just surrender everything to Him. He loves you with perfect care.

God Blessed Israel as Their King

Do you also remember that from Adam to Samuel, God's people had no earthly king? The LORD was their King directly. With God as their King, Noah was spared of God's wrath, Moses defeated the greatest military and Joshua took Jericho. They saw God's goodness and favor. However, the ungodly nations rebelled against God and His government. They made "man kings" to rule over them. These ungodly nations rejected God and set up a type of government based on Satan's ways, not God's laws. Then when Israel asked for a king during Samuel's judging, they rejected God as their King. This is why there is a danger when people drift from God's ways to rely on the inferior guidance of trusting in people. Can you look at this from God's perspective? What does God think? In 1 Samuel 8:7 God shares:

[Israel has] rejected Me, that I should not reign over them.

No country can afford to make this mistake. When Israel took their eyes off God, He gave them what they thought they wanted. Israel's first "man king" was Saul. Do you realize that everything looked right with Saul, except one thing? Saul's heart was not right with God. To the people, they saw Saul's father Kish, who was a mighty man of power, and

Saul, who was choice and handsome. In fact, Saul was the most handsome person in Israel. From Saul's shoulders upward, Saul was taller than any of the people (1 Samuel 9:1-2). The nation did not consult God and pray: What is Your will? That is why the people got what looked right in their own understanding. But being handsome doesn't necessarily make a just leader. Then when Saul disobeyed God, curses from sin came forth. The Amalekites troubled Israel when Saul did not remove them completely as God commanded. Saul also fought God's people and David internally in Israel. Israel missed God's blessings by trusting in man. Even with Congress, a president and courts, the USA is to trust in Jesus.

God told Saul to leave no remnant of the Amalekites, but Saul didn't obey. Saul eventually was killed by an Amalekite as a result of his rebellion. With God's mercy to Israel, God gave them David as King to replace Saul. David loved God. However, God rejected Saul. 2 Samuel 15:23 says:

...Because you have rejected the word of the LORD, He also has rejected you [Saul] from being king.

Jesus is the King of the Kingdom of God

Jesus is King of the Kingdom of God (1 Cor. 15:24). By acknowledging Jesus Christ as King of your life and of the USA you restore government to God's government and not man's ways. As a result, we have the light of God's Kingdom, instead of the darkness of the devil. Jesus taught the disciples to pray, "Your kingdom come. Your will be done on earth as it is in heaven" (Luke 11:2). Everything not of Jesus Christ is against God and will perish. Psalm 145:13 reminds us:

Your kingdom is an everlasting kingdom, and Your dominion endures throughout all generations.

Our government submitting to the LORD.
John Jay (second from left)

How to Daily Welcome Jesus
as King of the USA

It is easy to welcome Jesus as your King. All you have to do is to ask Him from your heart. Jesus loves Americans more than anyone else loves us. *No person compares to Jesus.* While our Founding Fathers set up a president, Congress and courts, we look to God to be these positions beyond the people (Isaiah 33:22). Our Founding Fathers' miraculous success stands as proof that they submitted to and trusted in the LORD and not people (Nahum 1:7, 2 Chron. 26:5 and Prov. 3:5-6). Signer of the Constitution, John Dickinson said:

> **Kings or parliaments could not give the rights essential to happiness... We claim them from a higher source – from the King of kings and Lord of all the earth... They are born with us, exist with us, and cannot be taken from us...**

Do you see how our Founding Fathers thought? They sought after God's best plans for the USA. They were

117

principled men who claimed their rights from God. They refused to give their God-given rights away. Isn't that how Jesus lived? He only did the Father's will.

God's model for a nation is found in the book of Judges, where He is King and godly men are judges. Let's trust God as our King and choose God-fearing men for government.

Yes. It Takes Faith, But those Living by Faith Are Blessed By God

If you look at the miracles in God's Word, there is a common theme. This theme is *faith in God*. This is why we ask Jesus to be King of the USA by faith. God is bigger than anything. He is the one we are to trust. Jesus explains that our faith to believe that we receive from God is a key for answered prayer. Notice Jesus says in Mark 11:24:

Therefore I say to you, whatever things you ask when you pray, believe that you receive them, and you will have them.

The USA Has No King But King Jesus

Since the earth is God's and He gives us our rights, He is our King. Our Christian nation is also in covenant with God: The LORD is the God of the USA and we are His people. Do you see that Jesus is rightly our King? He wants your heart. He loves you. He asks for every nation to welcome Him. Soon He will be honored by all, even His enemies who He will judge in righteousness. Psalm 10:16 says:

The LORD is King forever and ever; The nations have perished out of His land.

Will you live daily with Jesus as your King? The USA can't be blessed by God if we exclude Him. Let's also teach our churches and school children to make Jesus our King.

118

12

Twenty-one Ways to Pray for the USA

Father,

We exalt You as the God of the USA and we make Your laws our laws.

In Jesus' name. Amen.

What would God have us pray? This is a wise question to ask. Would you agree that God's objective is for the USA to welcome Him as our God, including to our homes, government, schools, courts and businesses? We are to live for God. If our nation has sin, then Proverbs 3:7 says we are to fear the LORD and depart from evil. Our Founding Fathers did. For example, we see this with the prayers of George Washington and John Adams and their calls for thanksgiving to God and national repentance from sin.

Two Objectives of Praying for Our Nation

Have you wondered how to have your prayers answered? In John 15:7 Jesus gives us a key to answered prayer. He tells us that God answers prayers based on His Word. Jesus says:

If you abide in Me, and My words abide in you, you will ask what you desire, and it shall be done for you.

By abiding, or dwelling, in Christ and by thinking on what the Holy Bible says, His desires become our desires. We crucify our flesh, which is our sinful nature. We set our minds on things above, not on things of the earth (Colossians 3:1-2). We distinguish between the holy and the unholy and our prayers are answered (Ezekiel 22:43). When we read the Holy Bible we learn God's will (2 Timothy 3:16-17). This gives us two prayer objectives for our nation.

Prayer Objective 1: For the USA to Exalt God
When we pray for our nation, we are to put God and His desires first. Isn't that what Jesus means when He says, "You shall love the LORD your God with all your heart, with all your soul, with all your mind, and with all your strength" (Mark 12:30)? We love God by lifting up Jesus. He is to be exalted. Psalm 46:10 and 47:7 say:

Be still, and know that I am God; I will be exalted among the nations, I will be exalted in the earth!

For God is the King of all the earth...

Prayer Objective 2: For God's Laws to Be Our Laws
Our prayers are to be a holy request and not an unholy request (Ezekiel 22:23). This means it is a righteous cause to pray for God's laws to be the USA's laws. God will answer this prayer. There is a big difference between the liberty of God and the bondage ungodly politicians bring. Have you seen

Abraham Lincoln Reading the Bible with His Son

the difference? God warned Israel, "that they may distinguish My service from the service of the kingdoms of the nations" (2 Chronicles 12:8). We are to keep our Founding Father's godly laws, not "change" them.

We Are Not to Pray Against God

Here is an illustration that reveals a common error. How would you pray if you knew there was a Christian girl and there was a man who did sinful things trying to be friends with her? The man said he was a Christian but had a record of doing the opposite of what God says. He also said he would help the girl financially and provide her protection. As a Christian, would you ignore the man's disobedience to God because he said he would help financially and with protection? Would you pray for the ungodly man to have wisdom and discernment knowing that he doesn't follow God? Would you ask God to help the ungodly man in his plans? Would you stay silent? And even though God warns about wolves in sheep's clothing and for Christians not to be unequally yoked with non-believers, would you tell the girl to obey the ungodly man? No, you wouldn't do any of this! *You would pray for the girl to avoid the person whom God identifies as evil.* You would bind the Satanic powers with the man, as Jesus says. Because the man refuses to obey God, you would tell the girl to "shake the dust off your feet" and reject him and move on as Jesus teaches to do. Proverbs 4:14 says:

Do not enter the path of the wicked, and do not walk in the way of evil.

With care for the girl, you would warn her about the ungodly man. You would remember that God sees if you don't warn her of the harm (Ezekiel 33:2-9). *Do you know that it is the same for the USA not to enter the path of politicians, businesses or "churches" who break God's laws?* The Holy Bible does not teach to pray for the ungodly to have wisdom. Instead we are to ask God to give us real Christian government, businesses and churches. We see that Peter, John and other godly people obeyed God. They didn't obey government that opposed God. Acts 4:18-20 explains:

[The council] called [Peter and John] and commanded them not to speak at all nor teach in the name of Jesus. But Peter and John answered and said to them, "Whether it is right in the sight of God to listen to you more than to God, you judge. For we cannot but speak the things which we have seen and heard."

122

Biblical Ways to Pray for the USA

After thanksgiving and praise, here are Biblical ways God says for you, your family and the government to pray.

Twenty-one Biblical Ways to Pray for the USA

Pray for every American and government servant to:

1. **Live in covenant: The LORD is the God of the USA and we are His people** *Psalm 33:12, 2 Corinthians 6:16*

2. **Love God with all our heart, soul, mind and strength** *Mark 12:30*

3. **Serve Jesus Christ–who is King of the USA** *Psalm 33:12, Psalm 47:7-8, Psalm 10:16, Phil. 2:11*

4. **Obey what God says in the Holy Bible** *2 Timothy 3:16-17, John 14:21*

5. **Love one another as Jesus loved us** *John 13:34*

6. **Seek first the Kingdom of God and His righteousness as a nation–in everything** *Matthew 6:33*

7. **Fear the LORD and depart from evil** *Isaiah 11:2, Psalm 33:8, Psalm 34:7, Psalm 10:15, Proverbs 3:7*, **including to:**

8. **Bless our children–train them in the Lord, with the Holy Bible and Christian prayer in school** *Eph. 6:4*

9. **Have changed hearts to love children and end abortion** *Psalm 127:3-4, Malachi 4:6*

10. **Remove foreign gods** *Exodus 20:3, Mark 12:30*

11. **Be sexually pure–obey God's creation of one man and one woman lifelong marriage, with abstinence before marriage**
    Leviticus 18, 1 Thessalonians 4:3-8, Hebrews 13:4

123

12. Have strong families–wives to submit to their own husbands as to the Lord, husbands to love their wives as Christ loved the church and children to obey their parents in the Lord, and to turn the heart of the fathers to the children and the heart of the children to their fathers *Eph. 5:22-6:3, Mal 4:6*, and

13. Pray publicly in Jesus' name as our Founding Fathers did–to know that God hears us *John 16:23*

14. Be a nation and government after God's own heart
1 Samuel 13:14

15. Seek God's counsel as a nation *Joshua 9:14*

16. Seek the peace of the USA *Jeremiah 29:7*
The Hebrew word for peace is Shalom and means: "Completeness in number, safety and soundness in body; welfare, health and prosperity; peace, quiet, tranquility and contentment; peace in friendship of relationships; peace with God in covenant; peace from war…"

17. Ask God for mercy, receiving forgiveness by the blood of Jesus Christ *Psalm 147:11, 1 John 1:7-9, Joel 2:12-14*

18. Cry out to God about abominations/sin in the USA and for oppression to end *Judges 3:9, Nehemiah 9:28-38*

19. Pray for national repentance, confess the USA's sins, ask God to create in the USA a clean heart and to convict the people of sin *Psalm 51,1 John 1:7-9*

20. Endeavor to keep the unity of the Spirit *Ephesians 4:3*

21. Ask God for God-fearing men to lead the USA in Christ (true shepherds / fathers) *Luke 10:2*

These prayers are God's will as they are from the Holy Bible. They exalt God and make His laws the USA's laws.

Correctly Pray "1 Timothy 2"

Do you know that an unBiblical prayer does not glorify God? Let's correct an error that is made with 1 Timothy 2 so the USA will see more of God's blessings. For example, think of a politician who sins against God with "separation of church and state," or abortion, or sexual and homosexual sin, or foreign gods. This is someone God and our Founding Fathers disapprove of and warn Americans to separate from (Psalm 1, 2 Chron. 19:2, 1 Cor. 5:13). Instead of repenting, this politician calls evil good and good evil. Then, someone at church or on TV says, "God says to pray for government". So they pray an unBiblical prayer like: "Father, we thank You for 'so and so ungodly person' and we ask You to give them wisdom and discernment and we ask You to bless them..." Stop! This type of prayer isn't of God. Here is why.

First, God says that the ungodly in government are because of a nation's sin. Government corruption is the fruit of sin. It is a judgment of God to lead us to national repentance. God says to pray for repentance, not to help the ungodly (2 Chron. 19:2). Tyranny occurs from letting sin into a nation as we saw in Nehemiah 9:34-37. To avoid tyranny, the USA is to live for God and repent from our sin. Notice Judges 4:1-3 says:

> **...the children of Israel again did evil in the sight of the LORD. So the LORD sold them into the hand of Jabin... And the children of Israel cried out to the LORD; for Jabin had... harshly oppressed the children of Israel.**

What did God look for? He looked for His people to cry out to Him in repentance. Notice no one prayed for the ungodly to have wisdom. Crying out is how God delivers His people. In Judges 3 we see multiple times the pattern: sin, judgment, crying out and deliverance. Judges 3:7-9 says:

125

> So the children of Israel did evil in the sight of the LORD. They forgot the LORD their God, and served the Baals and Asherahs. Therefore the anger of the LORD was hot against Israel, and He sold them into the hand of Cushan-Rishathaim king of Mesopotamia...
>
> When the children of Israel cried out to the LORD, the LORD raised up a deliverer for the children of Israel, who delivered them: Othniel the son of Kenaz, Caleb's younger brother.

The second reason why Christians aren't to pray for the ungodly to have wisdom is that God doesn't say to do so. This is because to fear God is a prerequisite to have wisdom. A non-Christian needs to be saved first. Proverbs 9:10 says:

> The fear of the LORD is the beginning of wisdom...

Instead, a Biblical prayer is: "Father, may the government fear You and depart from evil. In Jesus' name." Notice Moses did not pray for Pharaoh to have wisdom or for God to bless him. Pharaoh wasn't following God's ways, but oppressing God's people. Instead, God worked through Moses and Aaron to remove Pharaoh who refused correction (Exodus 8:6, 9:23, 14:27...). God wanted Israel free to serve Him, not to stay in oppression. God tells us to do what He says, not what an ungodly person says to do that is against God. Remember David didn't surrender to Saul. Also, when the antichrist is in power, God's people will not take the mark of the beast. For whoever takes the mark will be sent to hell with the antichrist, false prophet, the beast and all who refuse Jesus (Rev. 14:9-11). We aren't to share in the sins of others. When we look at 1 Timothy 2, we are to look at the context. This means to read before and after the section. 1 Timothy 1:3, 9-10 and 18-20 say:

...charge some that they teach no other doctrine... **the law is not made for a righteous person, but for the lawless and insubordinate, for the ungodly and for sinners for, the unholy and profane, for murderers of fathers and murderers of mothers, for manslayers, for fornicators, for sodomites, for kidnappers, for liars, for perjurers...**

This charge I commit to you... wage the good warfare, having faith and a good conscience, which some having rejected, concerning the faith have suffered shipwreck, of whom are Hymenaeus and Alexander, whom I delivered to Satan that they may learn not to blaspheme.

Do you notice that the focus here is God's law? 1 Timothy 1 shows that things like sex outside of marriage, liars and perjurers are breaking God's law. Timothy is charged to wage the good warfare and even to deliver the rebellious of God to Satan that they may learn not to blaspheme. This is the context when we *get* to 1 Timothy 2:1, which continues:

Therefore I exhort first of all that supplications, prayers, intercessions, and giving of thanks be made for all men, for kings and all who are in authority, that we may lead a quiet and peaceable life in all godliness and reverence.

What does this mean? God gives two reasons to pray "for all men, for kings and all who are in authority". They are:

1. That we may lead a quiet and peaceable life, and

2. In all godliness and reverence.

Who are the "we"? The "we" are Christians. What should the result of our prayers be? That Christians may lead a quiet

127

and peaceable life. How? The answer is: In all godliness and reverence–including peace, morality and righteousness. *God wants us to pray for government to be holy.* This is how to get Paul's stated result. We are to pray for government to keep God's laws that our Founding Fathers made. Christians are to pray for God's plan for marriage, ending government paid abortion and for children to have the Holy Bible and Christian prayer back in school. There are well-meaning Christians who miss God's objective. The rest of 1 Timothy 2 is like the first chapter. It talks about God's laws. When you pray for an ungodly person to make Jesus their Lord and Savior, don't let praying for the ungodly person distract you from praying for God to be exalted and for His laws to be our laws.

Exalt God and Make His Laws Our Laws

The Holy Bible reveals God's will. When you pray Biblical prayers, God will answer. He expects His people to pray wisely to help the righteous, not to help the unrighteous (2 Chronicles 19:2). Is exalting God your objective? Our Founding Fathers made it their objective. In 1780, Congress' official Proclamation of Thanksgiving and Prayer called to cause the knowledge of Christianity to spread. Congress' said:

> **Whereas it hath pleased Almighty God, the Father of all mercies... It is therefore recommended... to cause the knowledge of Christianity to spread all over the Earth.**

As Christians, we want everyone to know the love of God. This means our covenant Christian nation is to exalt God and make His laws our laws. Will you have this be your prayer focus? Let's pray so Christianity fills every part of the USA. As a strong Christian nation, then we can help others.

128

13
Seek God First in Politics

Father,

We seek first Your Kingdom and Your

righteousness in voting and politics. We ask You

for a God-fearing government.

In Jesus' name. Amen.

W hen Jesus said, "Seek first the kingdom of God and His righteousness," He meant for everything including politics (Matthew 6:33). Our Founding Fathers believed this and expect Americans to be faithful stewards with a strong Christian government in Christ.

Founding Fathers Say to Be Political Christians

Do you realize that our Founding Fathers showed us that to be an American means to be a political Christian as they were? Like John Jay who said to "select and prefer Christians for our rulers" and Noah Webster who taught Americans:

When you become entitled to exercise the right of voting for public officers, let it be impressed on your mind that God commands you to choose for rulers, "just [righteous] men who will rule in the fear of God."

The preservation of government depends on the faithful discharge of this Duty; if the citizens neglect their Duty and place unprincipled men in

office, the government will soon be corrupted; laws will be made, not for the public good so much as for selfish or local purposes; corrupt or incompetent men will be appointed to execute the Laws; the public revenues will be squandered on unworthy men; and the rights of the citizen will be violated or disregarded.

If government fails to secure public prosperity and happiness, it must be because the citizens neglect the Divine Commands, and elect bad men to make and administer the Laws.

Now, imagine the USA filled with Christians actively seeking God first in politics as Jesus said to do. Can you see the blessings that "just men who will rule in the fear of God" bring to the USA? What can your church do to require strong Christians for government as our Founding Fathers did? Be open to the Holy Spirit. God wants to inspire you in excellence. If someone in government is not willing to obey God, then shouldn't voters replace that person? And shouldn't pastors, who are shepherds, warn us of the ungodly?

Our Founding Fathers Discredited the Ungodly

Psalm 14:1 says, "The fool has said in his heart, 'There is no God.'" Our Founding Fathers made the distinction between the one who serves God and the one who doesn't. They believed the ungodly were to be avoided like Psalm 1 says. History shows that they discredited atheists and forbid them to be jurors. In 1831 the New York Spectator reported:

The court of common pleas of Chester county (New York), a few days since rejected a witness who declared his disbelief in the existence of God. The presiding judge remarked, that he had not

before been aware that there was a man living who did not believe in the existence of God; that this belief constituted the sanction of all testimony in a court of justice: and that he knew of no cause in a <u>Christian country</u>, where a witness had been permitted to testify without such belief.

Our Founding Fathers used the word "infidel" for one not believing in God. Infidel is an archaic word for unbelievers. Noah Webster defined infidel as "One who disbelieves the inspiration of the Scriptures, and the divine origin of Christianity". Supreme Court Justice Joseph Story told us:

<u>Infidels and pagans were banished</u> from the halls of justice as unworthy of credit.

George Washington knew firsthand how God won the revolution for our Christian nation, so he said:

The Hand of providence has been so conspicuous in all this, that he must be worse than an infidel that lacks faith, and more than wicked, that has not gratitude enough to acknowledge his obligations.

Do you see that our Founding Fathers taught the superiority of Christianity? The idea of a "brotherhood" of man doesn't exist with God. Adam fell in sin, so a non-Christian is lost in sin. But Jesus made redemption for sin. God wants every non-Christian to turn to Him. Remember Jesus will separate the sheep and the goats—those who follow Him and those who don't.

God Calls the USA to Vote for Godly Men

Are you encouraged that God wants to help us stay close with Him? He told kings to write a copy of God's law in a book. God expects government to know what He says in the Holy Bible (Deut. 17:18). Deuteronomy 17:19-20 gives the reasons why government is to obey God's Word. It says:

131

> **...and he shall read it [God's Word] all the days of his life, that he may learn to fear the LORD his God and be careful to observe all the words of this law and these statutes, that his heart may not be lifted above his brethren, that he may not turn aside from the commandment to the right hand or to the left, and that he may prolong his days...**

Exodus 18:21 talks about rulers. The verse says:

> **Moreover you shall select from all the people able men, such as fear God, men of truth, hating covetousness...**

A Christian has higher standards than others. We shouldn't vote based on outside appearance. We also can't vote for non-believers. God and our Founding Fathers warn Christians not to vote for a Mormon, atheist or anyone else with a different gospel or no gospel. Instead, we are to vote based on one's obedience to the LORD. This makes our nation blessed. Regarding voting, look at 1 Samuel 16:7, which says:

> **Do not look at his appearance or at his physical stature, because I have refused him. For the LORD does not see as man sees; for man looks at the outward appearance, but the LORD looks at the heart.**

In John 14:21 Jesus shows:

> **He who has My commandments and keeps them, it is he who loves Me.**

Now, look at these two quotes from Daniel Webster. In the first quote, see again how Webster emphasizes our Founding Fathers bringing Christian religion into all aspects of our nation including politics. Then in the second quote, he says that we are to scrutinize government. He says:

Our fathers were brought hither by their high veneration for the Christian religion... They sought to incorporate its principles with the elements of their society, and to <u>diffuse its [Christian religion] influence through all their institutions, civil, political, or literary.</u>

I fear that [Americans] may place too implicit a confidence in their public servants and fail properly to scrutinize their conduct; that in this way they may be made the dupes [easily deceived] of designing men and become the instruments of their own undoing.

Will You Vote for Godly People?

We should want to serve God in voting. Godly people bring God's blessings. Here are Biblical priorities:

Government Servants Qualifications: What to Look for

1. **Government Servants are to Love God with all their Heart, Soul, Mind and Strength** (*Mark 12:30, Exod. 18:21*)
   - Is the person God-fearing? Do they hate covetousness (desiring what others have)? Do they obey God?

2. **Government Servants are to Love the People of the USA as Jesus Loved Them** (*John 13:34*)

Your Part: Christian Keys for Voting

1. **Seek God Before Elections**
   - Prepare your heart to know what God wants. Ask God who to vote for and search God's Word. (James 1:5)

2. **Require God-Fearing Candidates**
   - Actively pray and require that only real Christians be in government, so we don't have hypocrites.

- Directly ask politicians:
  - Are you a Christian? 2 Chronicles 15:2 says, "The LORD is with you while you are with Him." What will you do to include Jesus in government?
  - What will you do to bring the Holy Bible and Christian prayer back to schools? Our Founding Fathers made this a priority. (Psalm 33:12, Eph. 6:4)
  - What will you do to end all funding of abortion and teach children abstinence? (Exod. 20:13, 1 Cor. 6:9-10)
  - What will you do to protect God's ordinance of marriage, so God does not judge the USA? (2 Peter 2:6)
  - Are you on the Lord's side or not? Why? (Exod. 32:26)
3. **Find Out How the Person Voted**
  - Look at the politician's history. Do they follow God's ways? Vote for those who obey God. (2 Chron. 19:2)
4. **Vote for God-Fearing People**
  - Look for godly character and families, people who seek God and search His Word. (1 Cor. 11:1, Exodus 18:21)

Romans 13 Doesn't Say to Blindly Submit To Government

Have you heard Romans 13 mistakenly taught to submit to all government laws–whether they are good or evil? Someone may say, "God says to submit to all government." Does He? Since it cost Jesus His life to redeem us from sin, how can it be God's will for us to submit to government sin or for churches to be silent about our nation's sin? Doesn't God oppose sin? Proverbs 17:15 and 13, and 2 John 9-11 say:

He who justifies the wicked, and he who condemns the just, both of them are an abomination to the Lord.

> Whoever transgresses and does not abide in the doctrine of Christ does not have God... If anyone comes to you and does not bring this doctrine, do not receive him into your house nor greet him; for he who greets him shares in his evil deeds.
>
> Whoever rewards evil for good, evil will not depart from his house.

As a Biblical foundation, look at these points:

1. **The Holy Bible teaches us not to submit to anyone, including government, that disobeys God,** and

2. **Our Founding Fathers did not submit to ungodly government disobeying God.**

Moses, the Hebrew midwives, David, Elijah, Daniel, Shadrach, Meshach and Abednego, Mary and Joseph, the wise men, Peter and John... all obeyed God and disobeyed ungodly government. For example, do you remember the Hebrew midwives disobeyed the king of Egypt, when he told them to break God's laws, by "aborting" (killing) the male children? By obeying God, He blessed them. Exodus 1:15-20 read:

> Then the king of Egypt spoke to the Hebrew midwives... "When you do the duties of a midwife for the Hebrew women, and see them on the birthstools, if it is a son, then you shall kill him..."
>
> But the midwives feared God, and did not do as the king of Egypt commanded them...
>
> And the midwives said to Pharaoh, "Because the Hebrew women are not like the Egyptian women; for they are lively and give birth before the midwives come to them." Therefore God dealt well with the midwives, and the people multiplied and grew very mighty. And so it was, because the

midwives feared God, that He provided households for them.

The wise men worshipping Jesus obeyed God and did not return to Herod after the king asked them to return (Matt. 2:1-12). Mary and Joseph fled to Egypt when the king wanted Jesus (Matt. 2:13-16). Also, Daniel disobeyed the king (Daniel 6). With this background, let's read Roman 13:1:

Let every soul be subject unto the higher powers. For there is no power but of God: the powers that be are ordained of God. (KJV)

Powers not under God's authority are illegitimate. Today, Americans celebrate our Founding Fathers civil disobedience to the tyranny of Great Britain on July 4th each year. When we get to Romans 13:3-4, notice the point not to submit to ungodly laws is again made. Instead, it is a just cause to do good works to God. These verses say:

For rulers are not a terror to good works, but to the evil... But if thou do that which is evil, be afraid; for he beareth not the sword in vain: for he is the minister of God, a revenger to execute wrath upon him that doeth evil. (KJV)

"Evil" is disobeying God. "Good" is obeying God. A "law" punishing a Christian for doing good is not of God. Notice God gives authority to punish those doing evil, but not to punish a Christian for doing good. The context of Romans 13:1-7 is to obey higher powers in good. Rulers are to exalt God and obey holy laws. If churches sit back to let ungodly laws replace godly laws, do they love God? If churches submit to the "state" and not God, do they love God? Have you seen lukewarm Christians not take a stand for righteousness? That is friendship with the world. But God says to convince, rebuke, exhort and speak up boldly for Him (2 Tim. 4:2).

Most politicians say they are a Christian. This is another reason why our nation should have no problem for God's laws to be our laws. Are some politicians true Christians, or are they hypocrites? Jesus tells us that by their fruit we will know if they are of God or not (Matthew 7:15-20). Jesus doesn't want us deceived. Wolves in sheep's clothing harm the USA. They limit our freedom and blessings. Also, notice God's anger toward the unrepentant in Psalm 34:16 and 10:15-16:

The face of the LORD is against those who do evil, to cut off the remembrance of them from the earth.

Break the arm [remove the power] of the wicked and the evil man; Seek out his wickedness until You find none. The LORD is King forever and ever; The nations have perished out of His land.

Rejecting the ungodly, our Founding Fathers said in our Declaration of Christian Independence:

We hold these truths to be self-evident, that all men are created equal [by God], that they are endowed by their Creator [the LORD] with certain unalienable Rights, that among these are Life, Liberty and the pursuit of Happiness. – That to secure these rights, Governments are instituted [under God] among Men, deriving their just powers from the consent of the governed, – That whenever any Form of Government becomes destructive of these ends [disobeys God], it is the Right of the People to alter or to abolish it, and to institute new Government [that will obey God]...

How can we defend ourselves from someone opposing Christ today? God says to contend for our faith (Jude 1:3). And Galatians 1:8-9 shows the Christian's attitude. Paul says:

137

But even if we, or an angel from heaven, preach any other gospel to you than what we have preached to you, let him be accursed... if anyone preaches any other gospel to you than what you have received, let him be accursed.

Someone may say, "Doesn't 1 Peter 2:7 say to honor the king?" However, honor doesn't mean to follow a person in sin. Also, remember the USA is unique and stands above ungodly nations. We do not have an earthly king. Jesus is our King. Jesus is the Word of God too (John 1:1). A president or Congress aren't a king. 1 Peter 2:7 shows our covenant Christian nation first honors God and the Holy Bible. Will you live to honor God? Are you looking at things from our covenant perspective like our Founding Fathers did, instead of a natural carnal perspective? Then after God we honor the laws of our Christian Constitution–which was written to serve God and His Word. By covenant Americans honor King Jesus and the His Word. Be careful not to let anyone deceive you otherwise. Israel fell for not honoring King Jesus.

So what about government servants? God says to follow them as they follow Christ (1 Corinthians 11:1). If a government servant sins against God or breaks their oath to uphold our Christian Constitution, then *they have disqualified themselves.* God considers them a lawbreaker. Are Christians supposed to help the ungodly break the law? Psalm 1 and the rest of the Bible say no. Remember our government is made of three equal branches which point to the LORD based on Isaiah 33:22. The USA is a Christian republic, not a democracy. Americans say, "...to the Republic for which it stands, one nation under God..." A strong Christian nation is God's highest goal for a nation, not a democracy. Democracies typically don't obey God and become filled with corruption.

Will You Not Enter the Path of the Wicked?

How can we have God's best plans politically? One key is not to enter the path of the wicked. Noah Webster warned of unprincipled men. Daniel Webster said not to be the "dupes of designing men". We go down the wrong path with ungodly politicians. Do you agree with God that His priorities–which the ungodly call "social issues" or "social conservatives"–are the number one focus for politics? The blessings follow as a result. For the elections the church is to bring God and His priorities to attention. Can you do this? God says to avoid those disobeying Him. Looking more at Prov. 4:14-15 we see:

> **Do not enter the path of the wicked, and do not walk in the way of evil. Avoid it, do not travel on it; Turn away from it and pass on.**

Is your loyalty to Jesus Christ above political parties? Are you aware that the Democrat Party now opposes God and approves of sin? A simple analysis shows they stand for abortion and homosexual sin which *God forbids.* Look at their voting record and national platform. The Democrat Party isn't what it used to be. Doesn't Prov. 4:14-15 tell Christians to turn away from the Democrat Party? If you have been a Democrat, then examine what they truly stand for. You have to decide if you will obey God or not (2 Chron. 19:2). Every political group is to obey God. If you work for Christ with other political groups, speak up that they "do not walk in the way of evil."

Continuously Rely on God

God is our Rock, Fortress and Deliverer (Psalm 18, Psalm 91). That is why we are to rely on God and not politicians. How many politicians promised they would fix the economy, protect our borders and didn't? Why vote for someone who has little care for our Christian nation? Also, God never intended for us to rely on people (John 2:24-25)? That leads to a weak military without blessings. 2 Chron. 16:7 says:

> **Because you have relied on the king of Syria, and have not relied on the LORD your God, therefore the army of the king of Syria has escaped from your hand.**

To rely on God is to put all your weight on God as your help. 2 Chronicles 16:8 promises God's faithful help. It says:

> **Were the Ethiopians and the Lubim not a huge army with very many chariots and horsemen? Yet, because you relied on the LORD, He delivered them into your hand.**

Likewise, no one in Israel delivered Israel from Goliath except David. Everyone else looked to men, but David looked to God. He knew God would help him. Will you look to God to make the USA a strong Christian nation? He always helps His people. This is God's best plan for the USA.

God Asks You to Speak Up For Him

With Jesus Christ dwelling in each Christian, we are to seek God first in politics. If pastors and Christians neglect to speak up for God, do you think the ungodly will? Imagine the blessings the USA can have with every pastor calling his church to pray the USA's Covenant with God™, registering his congregation to vote and instructing his congregation to vote for those who obey God. You also can find Christian voter's guides that show how candidates vote on issues. If every Christian votes for those who rule in the fear of God, then the USA will have more blessings. For more information on how to register to vote, see USAChristianMinistries.com.

14

The Church Leads the USA

Jesus wants you to know how important you are. He trusts Christians to lead the USA. Two questions for pastors and every Christian are: Do you want the same thing for the USA that God wants? And do you agree that the Holy Spirit gives Christians God's wisdom, goodness and love that a non-Christian doesn't have without Christ? Both God and our Founding Fathers set up the church to be in charge of the USA. We are stewards for Christ. This is why it is God's best plans for the church to lead our nation. Otherwise we have inferior ways of sin. Look at the 1643 New England Articles of Confederation. They give the aim of our Founding Fathers. As God's church, we have the same goal. The articles declare:

Whereas we all came into these parts of America with one and the same end and aim, namely, to advance the Kingdom of our Lord Jesus Christ and to enjoy the liberties of the Gospel...

The USA Needs God's Perfect Love and Hope

There is no greater love than Jesus Christ laying down His life on the cross to forgive our sins. This shows that only

Christians can bring God's love to our nation. Think of a youth lost in darkness or the person facing a challenge. Both need Jesus. Only Christians are rooted and grounded in love, able to comprehend the width and length and depth and height of Christ which passes knowledge (Ephesians 3:17-18). Furthermore, only Jesus gives grace, hope, peace, healing and reconciliation. He gives strength to the weak and unites families. In covenant we have the Everlasting Arms to help us. Deuteronomy 33:27 promises:

The eternal God is your refuge, and underneath are the everlasting arms...

The USA Needs God's Truth

Jesus says that Christians alone have God's truth. As a Christian, do you believe Jesus? In John 14:6 He says:

I am the way, the truth, and the life. No one comes to the Father except through Me.

Everyone needs Jesus. The Jamestown settlers came:

... in propagating of Christian Religion to such People, as yet live in Darkness and miserable Ignorance of the true Knowledge and Worship of God...

The USA Needs God's Blessings: Financial Prosperity, Protection, Freedom...

Only in Jesus is sin's curse removed and we have God's blessings instead (Galatians 3:13, Proverbs 10:22). Through Jesus Christ the USA has God's prosperity, protection and freedom and every good and perfect gift.

We saw our national anthem's author, Francis Scott Key, urge every patriot to "seek to establish for his country in the eyes of the world, such a character as shall make her not unworthy of the name of a Christian nation." He believed that Christians make the USA "the land of the free and home of the brave". When you sing our national anthem remember that Jesus gives our freedom and makes us brave to fight for Christian freedom. Congress approved our Christian national anthem–the Star Spangled Banner. The closing stanza is:

O, thus be it ever when freemen shall stand, between their loved home and the war's desolation! Blest with victory and peace, may the heav'n-rescued land praise the Power that hath made and preserved us a nation! Then conquer we must, when our cause it is just, and this be our motto: "In God is our trust" and the star-spangled banner in triumph shall wave O'er the land of the free and the home of the brave!

Jesus Gives Christians Authority of the USA

The good news of Jesus Christ surpasses everything else. With the Holy Spirit, every Christian has greater abilities than others–for with God all things are possible. Not only are Christians the most loving people through Jesus, we also have God's authority, truth and wisdom to lead the USA. God promises that what we bind will be bound and what we loose will be loosed (Matthew 18:18). As God's church, we are to pull down Satan's strongholds. 2 Corinthians 10:4-5 says:

...the weapons of our warfare are not carnal but mighty in God for pulling down strongholds, casting down arguments and every high thing that exalts itself against the knowledge of God...

In Matthew 28:18, Jesus equips the church to lead by giving us His authority. Notice He says:

143

All authority has been given to Me in heaven and on earth...

Do you see that Scripture says Christians have God's authority to lead the USA? Jesus commanded the church to make disciples of all nations, including our whole nation. We are to baptize and teach everyone to observe His commandments. Our Founding Fathers show that this includes our government, military and media yielding to Jesus (Matthew 28:19-20). In Matthew 16:18 Jesus says:

I will build my church; and the gates of hell shall not prevail against it.

The Church is the Salt and Light of the USA

The church not only has God's authority and commission to disciple our Christian nation, Jesus told His followers that we are the salt and light of the USA.

Jesus explains in Matthew 5:13:

You are the salt of the earth; but if the salt loses its flavor, how shall it be seasoned? It is then good for nothing but to be thrown out and trampled underfoot by men.

Salt is a preservative and gives taste as a seasoning. Christians are what keeps the USA from corruption. As salt, we bring God's Word and purpose to our nation. If Christians don't lead the USA in Christ, then they have lost their flavor.

Jesus gives our nation life. He is the light of the world. Without Jesus, the world is in darkness, full of evil deeds, corrupt and lost. Jesus describes the dark as where people do evil deeds (John 3:19). As His church, Christians are also the light of the world. Jesus says in John 8:12 and Matthew 5:14:

...I [Jesus] am the light of the world. He who follows Me shall not walk in darkness, but have the light of life.

You are the light of the world. A city that is set on a hill cannot be hidden.

John Adams shares the importance of pastors. He says:

It is the duty of the clergy to accommodate their discourses to the times, to preach against such sins as are most prevalent, and recommend such virtues as are most wanted.

Without the church boldly leading, darkness comes to the USA. The Pilgrims used the phrase "city upon a hill" for America. Will you speak up for national repentance? Our nation needs Jesus. He is the light of the USA.

God's Word is the USA's Foundation

Do you remember Jesus speaking of the man who built his house, dug deep and laid the foundation on the rock and the other man who built without a foundation? Jesus said the rock is the Holy Bible. Unless we build on God's Word, then when the storms come we will fall. In Luke 6:47-49 Jesus explains:

Whoever comes to Me, and hears My sayings and does them, I will show you whom he is like: He is like a man building a house, who dug deep and laid the foundation on the rock. And when the flood arose, the stream beat vehemently against that house, and could not shake it, for it was founded on the rock. But he who heard and did nothing is like a man who built a house on the earth without a foundation, against which the stream beat vehemently; and immediately it fell. And the ruin of that house was great.

145

Build the USA on the Rock of Christ

Jesus Christ Gives A Hedge of Protection Around the USA

How can you do your part to build the USA on the Holy Bible as our nation's foundation? Everything not built on Christ will be lost. Like Nehemiah rebuilding the walls of Jerusalem, where can you build our foundation on Christ? Helpful questions are: Where is the USA obeying God? Where is the USA disobeying God? Psalm 11:3 & 125:3 say:

If the foundations are destroyed, what can the righteous do?

For the scepter of wickedness shall not rest on the land allotted to the righteous, lest the righteous reach out their hands to iniquity.

146

Christian Fathers Lead the USA

What made the USA so blessed? It is godly pastors and Christians inspiring America in Christ that gave our nation birth. A true father in the Lord, who is also called a shepherd:

1. **Intercedes with God to forgive the USA (Ezekiel 22:30, Psalm 106:23), and**
2. **Teaches the people the Holy Bible (Numbers 14:19).**

Christian leaders are to love every Christian and to protect the Christian church in the USA. If you are a leader, stay faithful to Jesus. If you need His counsel and power, just ask and it will be given to you. He knows you love Him. We see that when Moses, Samuel and others prayed for their nation, God answered with mercy. Hebrews 11 shows that anything can be done by faith. Will you believe for God's best plans? God doesn't have a fatalistic plan. God is in charge, not the devil. Faith is acting on God's Word. God will answer your cry for the USA to be holy and to have true fathers (1 John 2:14).

The Church is to Restrain the USA From Evil

When the children of Israel turned from God in Exodus 32, verse 25 explains the reason was *Aaron did not restrain the people.* However, Moses quickly restrained the people by dividing the people and saying, "who is on the Lord's side?" It is helpful for Christians to ask this question too when they talk with others. We also find that the church of Thyatira did not restrain the people. The church permitted God's people to be led astray by a woman to worship idols and commit sexual sin (Revelation 2:20). In contrast, Nehemiah obeyed God and boldly restrained the people from evil. Nehemiah 13:1 shows:

> **So I contended with the rulers, and said, "Why is the house of God forsaken?" And I gathered them together and set them in their place.**

147

God's Calls the USA to be a Strong Christian Nation

Covenant Nation		Broken Covenant Nation
Built on God		Built Without God
God is our Foundation	OR	No Foundation
Holy: Live for God		Unholy: Live for Self

Blessed Nation	Cursed Nation
Righteousness and Truth	**Unrighteousness and Lies**
Life	**Wages of Sin (Death)**
- Love	- Self seeking
- Strong Families	- Broken Families
Liberty	**Tyranny**
- Christian Freedom	- Controlled
- Honesty & Integrity	- Corruption
Happiness	**Unhappiness**

Include God in Homes & Government	Broken Covenant Children
Holy Bible & Christian Prayer in School	Whatever Abortions - 53 Million
Pro Life – End Abortion	Seems Fornication, Adultery &
1 Man 1 Woman Marriage	"Right" Homosexual Sin
God's Laws Holiness	Lawless Other Sin

GOD & HIS WORD	**SATAN & SIN**
Covenant Relationship With God	Rejected By God
Forgiveness	Judgment
Protection	No Protection
Deliverance	Defeated

Two Different Destinies

God's Way to Handle Correction

Correction is part of leading. It is a responsibility of God's church. So let's look Biblically how God says to correct. If the person is a Christian we are to pray for them, providing they are not committing sin leading to death. 1 John 5:13 says:

148

If anyone sees his brother sinning a sin which does not lead to death, he will ask, and He will give him life for those who commit sin not leading to death. There is sin leading to death. I do not say that he should pray about that.

Jesus calls each person to repent. Matt. 18:15-17 says:

Moreover if your brother sins against you, go and tell him his fault between you and him alone. If he hears you, you have gained your brother. But if he will not hear, take with you one or two more, that "by the mouth of two or three witnesses every word may be established." And if he refuses to hear them, tell it to the church. But if he refuses even to hear the church, let him be to you like a heathen and a tax collector.

As Christians, we follow what Jesus says. However, for those who will not listen to Him, Jesus teaches in Mark 6:11:

And whoever will not receive you nor hear you, when you depart from there, shake off the dust under your feet as a testimony against them.

If a politician refuses correction, Jesus says the USA is to "shake the dust off our feet," or reject them, and replace them with one who follows God. Because most politicians publicly say they are a Christian, 1 Corinthians 5:11-13 teaches to not associate with them if they disobey God. The Holy Bible says:

But now I have written to you not to keep company with anyone named a brother, who is sexually immoral, or covetous, or an idolater, or a reviler, or a drunkard, or an extortioner–not even to eat with such a person... put away (separate) from yourselves that wicked person.

149

We learn more about God's power in 1 Corinthians 5:5 and 1 Timothy 1:20. Paul teaches to deliver those who refuse correction to Satan. This is a loving action as the non-repentant person may suffer in hell. Notice 1 Corinthians 5:3-5 teaches:

> **For I indeed, as absent in body but present in spirit, have already judged... In the name of our Lord Jesus Christ, when you are gathered together, along with my spirit, with the power of our Lord Jesus Christ, deliver such a one to Satan for the destruction of the flesh, that his spirit may be saved in the day of the Lord Jesus.**

God cares for everyone to live holy. He uses His people to remove those refusing correction. Examples include: Moses with Pharaoh, Psalm 149, crying out to Him (Judges 3:9) and others. Paul taught in 1 Corinthians 16:22 and Galatians 1:8-9:

> **If any man love not the Lord Jesus Christ, let him be Anathema [accursed] Maranatha. (KJV)**
>
> **But even if we, or an angel from heaven, preach any other gospel to you than what we have preached to you, let him be accursed. As we have said before, so now I say again, if anyone preaches any other gospel to you than what you have received, let him be accursed.**

Leading as God's Powerful Church

If you want to show that you love God, then build the USA's foundation on the Holy Bible (John 1:1, Joshua 1:8). Christians are to make disciples of the whole nation. God calls for Christians to lead. As a Christian, you are the salt and the light of the USA. 1 John 3:2 assures God's grace and power to you. It shows that Christians are God's leaders because:

> **Beloved, now we are children of God...**

15
Action Plan: Your Assignment

Father,

I give myself to You. Help me strengthen my life,
my family and the USA in Christ.

In Jesus' name. Amen.

What has following Jesus done for the USA? The answer is everything that is good about our nation (James 1:17). The USA you desire–walking remarkably close with God and filled with His love, prosperity, peace and freedom–is because of Jesus (John 10:10). What has following sin done to the USA? The answer is every curse that you don't like about our nation.

Our Founding Fathers established our unique covenant Christian nation. This covenant is to all generations and it is unbreakable. Obeying it is how God dwells among us. A Christian nation is the nation God blesses (2 Cor. 3:17). The keys to fix the economy, strengthen national security and to restore freedom are to exalt God and to make His laws our laws. As you seek God for what you can do for Christ in the USA, have confidence He will direct you. One obedient person can bring God's plan for the USA (Ezekiel 22:30). How will you get involved in the USA for Christ? And what will your church do to strengthen our Christian nation?

First: Join the Covenant

There are several areas you can help with. First, will you agree that the LORD is the God of the USA? Pray:

The USA's Covenant With God™

Father,

As a Christian nation dedicated to You, we affirm our covenant:

- **You, the LORD, are the God of the USA and we are Your people. Jesus is our King. We obey what You say in the Holy Bible.**

- **We love You with all our heart, soul, mind and strength.**

- **We love one another as Jesus loved us.**

- **We ask You to forgive our sins by Jesus' sacrifice.**

In Jesus' name. Amen. *Psalm 33:12, Mark 12:30, John 13:34, 2 Chronicles 15:12, 1 John 1:7*

See www.USAChristianMinistries.com for tools.

Permission is given to reprint and pray The USA's Covenant with God™ in handouts, articles and on TV and radio provided the prayer is given for free and includes a reference to USAChristianMinistries.com. For other uses contact USA Christian Ministries to inquire about permission.

Second: Strengthen Our Nation in Christ

Here are key ways to make a strong Christian nation:

1. Teach everyone the USA's Covenant with God™

- Hold a church service and also a home family dedication.
    1. Read our Founding Fathers' Christian quotes.
    2. Confess the USA's sins to God - national repentance.
    3. Pray the covenant prayer.

- Put the covenant on your desktop or refrigerator and get a wristband at www.USAChristianMinistries.com.

2. Share: *Making a Strong Christian Nation*

- Give *Making a Strong Christian Nation* to every Christian and pastor you are able to, so more can get involved.

3. Decide if you are on the Lord's Side? Then live for God:
- Confess Jesus to be your Lord (Philippians 2:11).
- Call on Jesus to be your Savior (John 3:16, Rom. 10:13).
- Agree that the Holy Bible is God's Word, inerrant and infallible (2 Timothy 3:16-17).
- Pray and read the Holy Bible every day. Read a chapter or more in the morning and evening.
- Memorize Bible verses and think about them each day.
- Pray as a family. Pray before meals.
- See Strengthen Our Families in Christ tools at: USAChristianMinistries.com.

4. Answer God's Call for National Repentance
   1) Agree with God that the USA's sins are to end:
- Lukewarm church and efforts to break covenant
- The 1947 lie of "separation of church and state"
- Taking the Holy Bible and Christian prayer out of schools
- 53+ million abortions
- Not honoring our father and mother
- Condoning sexual and homosexual sin
- Serving money (mammon)
- Voting for ungodly people
- Putting trust in something other than God
- Not seeking God's counsel
- Unbelief that God will save our Christian nation
- Divided instead of keeping the unity of the Spirit

153

- Allowing foreign gods
- Selfish individualism
- Other sins...

2) Get Active to End the Above Sins-Repent as a nation:
- Pray to end these sins and for our hearts to love God
- Speak up for Jesus
- Make God's laws the USA's laws. Combine Christian churches and government. Remove the lie of "separation of church and state".
  - Bring the Holy Bible and Christian prayer back to schools.
  - Help do what you can to end abortion.
  - Stand up for God by keeping God's marriage only. One man and one woman for life.
  - Pastors: Preach the USA is to have God's laws be our laws.

5. Prioritize to Remove Root Issues (Sin) More than Fruit Judgment Issues
- Call for national repentance of sins in #4 above)
- God says obeying Him causes economic prosperity, lower taxes, peace, freedom and other blessings (2 Corinthians 3:17, Deuteronomy 28, Leviticus 26, Psalm 33:12).
- Sin causes the curses of economic decline, high taxes, wars, loss of freedoms... (Galatians 6:7-8, Deut. 28, Lev. 26, Nehemiah 9:33-38, Lev. 18, Judges 3-4).
- Tea Party and others concerned about the economy, taxes, freedom...
  o Prioritize to remove sins (the real root issues).
  o Understand corruption issues are consequences (fruit).

6. Build the USA on the Foundation of Jesus Christ
- Build the USA's foundation on the rock of the Holy Bible.
- Repent from places built without a foundation.

7. Month of Celebrations

- Make products (books, songs, videos...), write articles, share at church, youth groups, schools, bulletins...
  - January: *Seek God First in Politics Month* Matt. 6:33
  - February: *Sexual Purity Awareness Month* 1 Thess. 4:3-8
  - March: *Month of the Bible* 2 Timothy 3:16-17
  - April: End Abortion / *Abortion Recovery Awareness Month* Hebrews. 9:14
  - May: *God in USA History Month* Psalm 33:12
  - June: *Honor Your Father and Mother Month* Eph. 6:1-2
  - July: *Affirm the USA's Covenant with God^{TM}* Psalm 33:12
  - August: *Strengthen Your Family in God Month* Ephesians 5:22-6:4
  - September: *Holy Bible and Christian Prayer In Schools Awareness Month* Ephesians 6:4
  - October: *Give a Bible Away Month* Matt. 28:19-20
  - November: *Month of Thanksgiving to God* Psalm 107
  - December: *Know the Biblical Jesus Month* John 14:6
- Sign up for monthly email at: USAChristianMinistries.com.

8. Pray and Fast for the USA

- Wednesdays pray and fast as your health/doctor allows.
- Pastors: Call your church to regularly pray for the USA.
- Form *2 Chronicles 7:14 Prayer Group(s)*.
- Daily pray the USA exalts God & makes His laws our laws.
- Sign up for daily email at: USAChristianMinistries.com.

9. Encourage Every Christian to Vote for Godly People

- Ask God in faith for God-fearing candidates.
- Pastors: Speak up politically. Teach to vote for God-fearing candidates. Register every Christian to vote.

10. Run for Congress, City Council, School Board...

- Seek God, so you can do the Father's will (Col. 1:9).
- Organize your support team, campaign and be elected.

155

11. Join the USA's Thanksgiving Choir (Neh. 12:31)
• Daily praise and worship God–sing one or more songs.
• Lead and encourage others in daily thanksgiving to God.

12. Bible Blitz USA (Every Week)
• Fill the USA with God's Word. Share weekly Bible verses and God in USA history quotes on the Internet, bulletins...
• Sign up for weekly email at: USAChristianMinistries.com.

13. Display the USA's National Motto: In God We Trust
• Share at schools, government buildings, speeches, media...
• Tools at: USAChristianMinistries.com.

14. Make Disciples of the USA
• Teach God's Word. Stick to the Bible (Matthew 28:20).
• Take up your cross and follow Jesus (John 14:6).

How Will You Help Unite the USA in Christ?

Are you ready for the proven benefits of a strong Christian nation? Perhaps, you and your church can write a monthly/yearly plan of what you can do. Let's live for God. What have you learned in this book? How has God spoken to you to make the USA a strong Christian nation? Your efforts in Christ will make a difference. God bless you and God bless the USA! As a Christian family, let's welcome God with all our hearts by covenant affirming:

The LORD is the God of the USA and We Are His People.

ॐ✦ॐ

The following two bonus books give 100 ways how to live God's Greatest Commandments from the Holy Bible.

The Prayer of Salvation and Study Guide are afterwards.

156

BONUS BOOK
100 Ways to Love God

Father,

I love You with all my heart, with all my soul,

with all my mind, and with all my strength.

In Jesus' name. Amen.

Jesus gave us the first of God's two Greatest Commandments in Mark 12:30. He said:

You shall love the LORD your God with all your heart, with all your soul, with all your mind, and with all your strength.

Here are one hundred ways how to love God:

100 Ways to Love God

1. **Love God with all your heart (innermost being)**
   Mark 12:30

2. **Love God with all your soul (emotions, will…)**
   Mark 12:30

3. **Love God with all your mind (thoughts, intellect…)**
   Mark 12:30

4. **Love God with all your strength (what you do, how you live…)** *Mark 12:30*

5. **Seek not your own things, but the things which are of Christ Jesus** *Philippians 2:20*

6. **Draw near to God** *James 4:8*

7. **Tell God that He is the God of the USA and we are His people** *2 Corinthians 6:16, Psalm 33:12*

8. **Ask Jesus to be King of your life, family and the USA** *Isaiah 33:22, Philippians 2:11*

9. **Obey what God says in the Holy Bible as interpreted by Jesus** *2 Timothy 3:16, Matthew 28:20*

10. **Make disciples** *Matthew 28:19-20*

11. **Abide in Christ** *John 15:7*

100 Ways to Love God (Continued)

12. **Know God as Elohim, "Creator"** *Genesis 1:1*

13. **Know God as Jehovah, "my Lord God"**
Genesis 2:7

14. **Think of how God has shown you grace** *Eph. 2:8-9*

15. **Tell others Jesus Christ rose from the dead**
John 11:25, 1 Corinthians 15

16. **Don't add to or take away from the Holy Bible**
Revelation 22:18-19

17. **Vote only for people who obey God**
2 Chronicles 19:2, Psalm 1, 2 Samuel 23:3

18. **Put away (separate) from yourselves the wicked
person** *1 Corinthians 5:13*

19. **Obey God** *John 14:21*

20. **Have no other gods before the LORD your God**
Exodus 20:3

21. **Break all ties with the occult**
Leviticus 19:31, Leviticus 20:6

22. **Live for God** *Galatians 2:20*

23. **Know God as Adonai, "Master and Lord"**
Genesis 18:2

100 Ways to Love God (Continued)

24. **Tell God you love Him** *Psalm 116:1*

25. **Love every Christian** *1 John 3:14*

26. **Walk in the unity of the Spirit** *Ephesians 4:3*

27. **Hate evil** *Psalm 97:10, 1 Thessalonians 5:22*

28. **Pray an hour or more with Jesus** *Matthew 26:40*

29. **Know God as Jehovah Jireh, "the Lord my Provider"** *Genesis 22:14, Philippians 4:19*

30. **Believe God and Jesus Whom He Sent** *Romans 4:3*

31. **Give thanksgiving to God** *Psalm 100:4, 1 Thessalonians 5:18*

32. **Praise God** *Psalm 150, Psalm 100:4*

33. **Thank God for giving us His Word–the Holy Bible** *2 Timothy 3:16-17, Psalm 119*

34. **Do not love the world or the things in the world** *1 John 2:15-17*

35. **Know God as El Shaddai, "God Almighty, my Supply, my Nourishment"** *Genesis 17:1*

36. **Do not take the name of the Lord your God in vain** *Exodus 20:7*

100 Ways to Love God (Continued)

37. **Exalt Jesus Christ** *Philippians 2:9*

38. **Feed His sheep** *John 21:17, 1 Peter 5:2-3*

39. **Delight yourself in the LORD** *Psalm 37:4*

40. **Go and sin no more** *John 8:11*

41. **Know God as Jehovah Rophe, "the Lord who heals"** *Exodus 15:26*

42. **Pray for every American to love God, with all their heart, soul, mind and strength** *Mark 12:30*

43. **Seek first the Kingdom of God and His righteousness** *Matthew 6:33*

44. **Tell others that only the Holy Bible is God's Word** *2 Timothy 3:16-17*

45. **Seek God's way of escape out of temptation** *1 Corinthians 10:13*

46. **Know God as Jehovah Nissi, "the Lord my Victory"** *Exodus 17:15*

47. **Enter into the Holy of Holies by the blood of Jesus** *Hebrews 10:19*

48. **Expect God's miracles** *Mark 10:27*

100 Ways to Love God (Continued)

49. **Press toward the goal for the prize of the upward call of God in Christ Jesus** *Philippians 3:14*

50. **Sing a new song to God** *Psalm 33:3*

51. **Read your Bible in the morning and evening** *Joshua 1:8*

52. **Tell others that you are not ashamed of the Gospel of Christ** *Romans 1:16*

53. **Praise the Lord for His mercy endures forever** *2 Chronicles 20:21*

54. **Rejoice in the Lord always** *Philippians 4:4*

55. **Humble yourselves under the mighty hand of God** *1 Peter 5:5-6*

56. **Expect God to reward you for diligently seeking Him** *Hebrews 11:6*

57. **Thank God for His faithfulness** *Psalm 89:8*

58. **Speak to your mountain and tell it to be removed** *Mark 11:23, Matthew 17:20*

59. **Know God as your Father** *Luke 11:2*

60. **Cleanse your way–hide God's Word in your heart so you may not sin against God** *Psalm 119:9-11*

100 Ways to Love God (Continued)

61. **Let God embrace you when you return to Him**
    Luke 15:17-24

62. **Sigh and cry over the abominations that are done within the USA** *Ezekiel 9:4*

63. **Rely on God** *2 Chronicles 16:7-8*

64. **Thank Jesus that your name is written in the Lamb's Book of Life** *Revelation 21:27, Psalm 87:6*

65. **Fear God** *Revelation 14:7, Proverbs 1:7*

66. **Believe that with God all things are possible** *Mark 10:27*

67. **Finish your race with joy** *Acts 20:24, 2 Timothy 3:7*

68. **Know God as Jehovah Tsidkenu, "the Lord who is our Righteousness"** *Jeremiah 23:5-6*

69. **Trust in the Lord with all your heart**
    Proverbs 3:5-6

70. **Believe every word in the Holy Bible**
    Isaiah 55:11, 2 Timothy 3:16-17

71. **Ask the Holy Spirit to help you** *John 14:16, 26*

72. **Know God as Jehovah Shalom, "the Lord my peace"** *Judges 6:24*

163

100 Ways to Love God (Continued)

73. **Be led by the Spirit** *Romans 8:14*

74. **Withdraw from every brother who walks disorderly** *2 Thessalonians 3:6*

75. **Thank God that: for by grace you have been saved through faith, and that not of yourselves; it is the gift of God, not of works, lest anyone should boast** *Ephesians 2:8-9*

76. **Seek and do the Father's will** *Matthew 7:21*

77. **Know God as Jehovah Rohi, "my Shepherd"** *Psalm 23:1*

78. **Do a good work for Jesus in love for Him, like the woman pouring the expensive, fragrant oil on Jesus' head** *Matthew 26:6-12*

79. **Seek those things which are above, where Christ is, sitting at the right hand of God** *Colossians 3:1*

80. **Remember the Sabbath day, to keep it holy** *Exodus 20:8*

81. **Hate divorce** *Malachi 2:16*

82. **Take up the cross, and follow Jesus** *Mark 10:21*

83. **Rejoice in Christ Jesus** *Philippians 3:3, 1 Thessalonians 5:16*

100 Ways to Love God (Continued)

84. **Know Jesus as your friend** *John 15:15*

85. **Love Jesus more than father, mother, son or daughter** *Matthew 10:37*

86. **Do the will of God from the heart** *Ephesians 6:6*

87. **Look unto Jesus, the author and finisher of our faith** *Hebrews 12:2*

88. **Know God as Jehovah Shammah, "the Lord is there"** *Ezekiel 48:35*

89. **Be pure in heart** *Matthew 5:8*

90. **Hunger and thirst after righteousness** *Matthew 5:6*

91. **Keep God's Word** *John 14:34*

92. **Pray the Lord of the harvest to send out laborers into His harvest** *Luke 10:2*

93. **Whatever things you ask when you pray, believe that you receive them, and you will have them** *Mark 11:24*

94. **Confess Jesus before others** *Matthew 10:32*

95. **Think of where God has shown you mercy** *Ephesians 2:4, Hebrews 4:16*

100 Ways to Love God (Continued)

96. **Whatever you do, do it heartily, as to the Lord and not to men** *Colossians 3:23*

97. **Contend earnestly for the faith** *Jude 3*

98. **Watch and pray** *Matthew 26:40-41*

99. **Be still before God** *Isaiah 30:15, Psalm 46:10*

100. **Read the whole Bible, asking God to help you understand what He is saying** *2 Timothy 3:16-17*

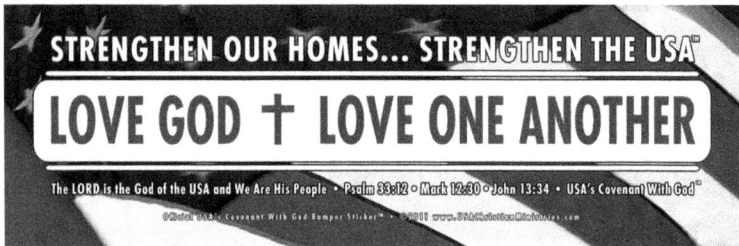

See: www.USAChristianMinistries.com for sharing tools

BONUS BOOK
100 Ways to Love One Another

Father,

Jesus laid down His life for me on the Cross.

I want to love others as Jesus loved me.

In Jesus' name. Amen.

By this we know love, because Jesus laid down His life for us (1 John 3:16). Now as Christians we are to do the same. Jesus gives us the second of God's Greatest Commandments in John 13:34. He says:

Love one another; as I have loved you, that you also love one another.

Here are one hundred ways how to love one another, strengthening our homes and the USA:

100 Ways to Love One Another

1. As Jesus has loved you, love one another
   John 13:34

2. Forgive one another as Christ forgave you
   Colossians 3:13

3. We also ought to lay down our lives for the
   brethren *1 Corinthians 13:4*

4. If your brother sins against you, go and tell him his
   fault between you and him alone–If he hears you,
   you have gained your brother *Matthew 18:15,
   James 5:19*

5. Suffer long and be kind *1 Corinthians 13:4*

6. Do not envy *1 Corinthians 13:4*

7. Do not parade yourself *1 Corinthians 13:4*

8. Do not be puffed up *1 Corinthians 13:4*

9. Do not behave rudely *1 Corinthians 13:5*

10. Do not seek your own *1 Corinthians 13:5,
    Philippians 2:1*

11. Do not be provoked *1 Corinthians 13:5*

12. Think no evil *1 Corinthians 13:5*

100 Ways to Love One Another (Continued)

13. **Do not rejoice in iniquity** *1 Corinthians 13:6*

14. **Rejoice in the truth** *1 Corinthians 13:6*

15. **Bear all things** *1 Corinthians 13:7*

16. **Believe all things** *1 Corinthians 13:7*

17. **Hope all things** *1 Corinthians 13:7*

18. **Endure all things** *1 Corinthians 13:7*

19. **Never fail** *1 Corinthians 13:8*

20. **Give a Holy Bible to someone** *Matthew 28:19-20*

21. **Look out not only for your own interests, but also for the interests of others** *Philippians 2:4*

22. **Pursue love** *1 Corinthians 14:1*

23. **Bear one another's burdens, and so fulfill the law of Christ** *Galatians 6:2*

24. **Comfort one another with Scriptures on Christ's return** *1 Thessalonians 4:18*

25. **Rejoice with those who rejoice** *Romans 15:15*

26. **Weep with those who weep** *Romans 15:15*

100 Ways to Love One Another (Continued)

27. Be a Good Samaritan and help people in need (with wisdom) *Luke 10:30-37*

28. Whoever compels you to go one mile, go with him two *Matthew 5:41*

29. Show mercy *Matthew 5:7*

30. Give a cup of water to the thirsty in Jesus' name *Matthew 10:23*

31. Let your speech always be with grace, seasoned with salt *Colossians 4:6*

32. Be a peacemaker *Matthew 5:9*

33. Do not render evil for evil *1 Thessalonians 5:15*

34. Do not commit adultery *Exodus 20:14*

35. Let your light so shine before men *Matthew 5:16*

36. Share what you have (this world's goods) with your brother in need *1 John 3:17*

37. Everyone who loves is born of God and knows God *1 John 4:7*

100 Ways to Love One Another (Continued)

38. **Rule your own house well, having your children in submission with all reverence** *1 Timothy 3:4*

39. **Edify one another** *1 Thessalonians 5:11*

40. **Do not show partiality** *James 2:4*

41. **Give food to the hungry** *Matthew 25:31-45*

42. **Exhort one another daily** *Hebrews 3:13*

43. **Walk in love** *Ephesians 5:2*

44. **Let your gentleness be known to all** *Philippians 4:5*

45. **Don't be quarrelsome** *1 Timothy 3:3*

46. **Minister to the sick and those in prison**
    Matthew 25:31-45, Hebrews 13:3

47. **Pray for ministers to open their mouth boldly to make known the mystery of the Gospel**
    Ephesians 6:19

48. **Share John 3:16 with someone** *John 3:16*

49. **Do not steal** *Exodus 20:15, Ephesians 4:28*

50. **Managers: Do not threaten, or show partiality**
    Ephesians 6:9

100 Ways to Love One Another (Continued)

51. **Pray for your family and church to comprehend what is the width and length and depth and height of Christ's love** *Ephesians 3:18-19*

52. **Don't be greedy for money** *1 Timothy 3:3*

53. **Have sincere love of the brethren** *1 Peter 1:22*

54. **Visit orphans and widows in their trouble** *James 1:27*

55. **Workers: Be obedient to your employers, with fear and trembling, in sincerity of heart, as to Christ...** *Ephesians 6:5-8*

56. **Be rooted and grounded in love** *Ephesians 3:17*

57. **Pursue love** *1 Corinthians 14:1*

58. **Warn others about wolves in sheep's clothing** *Matthew 7:15-20*

59. **Let no corrupt word proceed out of your mouth, but what is good for necessary edification, that it may impart grace to the hearers** *Ephesians 4:29*

60. **Wives, submit to your husbands, as to the Lord, and respect them** *Ephesians 5:22, 33*

61. **Husbands, love your wives, just as Christ loved the church** *Ephesians 5:25*

100 Ways to Love One Another (Continued)

62. **Children, obey your parents in the Lord, for this is right** *Ephesians 6:1, Exodus 20:12*

63. **Bear with the scruples of the weak** *Romans 15:1*

64. **Add to your faith... brotherly kindness** *2 Peter 1:5-7*

65. **Everyone who loves God who begot Jesus Christ also loves him who is begotten of Him** *1 John 5:1*

66. **In honor give preference to one another** *Romans 12:10*

67. **Pray always with all prayer and supplication in the Spirit, being watchful to this end with all perseverance and supplication for all the saints** *Ephesians 6:18*

68. **Be tender hearted** *Ephesians 4:32*

69. **Pray for your brother to repent, if you see him sinning a sin not leading to death** *1 John 5:13*

70. **Pray for Christians to know the love of Christ which passes knowledge** *Ephesians 3:19*

71. **Speak to one another in psalms and hymns and spiritual songs, singing and making melody in your heart to the Lord** *Ephesians 5:19, Colossians 3:16*

100 Ways to Love One Another (Continued)

72. **Be like-minded toward one another, according to Christ Jesus** *Romans 15:5*

73. **Pray and fast to rebuke demons and cure others** *Matthew 17:18-21*

74. **First remove the plank from your own eye, and then you will see clearly to remove the speck from your brother's eye** *Matthew 7:3-5*

75. **Do not grumble against one another** *James 5:9*

76. **Do not receive into your house anyone who preaches anything other than the Gospel of Jesus Christ** *2 John 10-11*

77. **Be hospitable, including to entertain strangers (with wisdom)** *Timothy 3:3, Hebrews 13:2*

78. **Love God and keep His commandments** *1 John 5:2*

79. **As you have received a gift, minister it to one another** *James 4:10*

80. **Have compassion on those who continue with Jesus and have need** *Mark 8:2*

81. **Lay down your life for the brethren** *1 John 3:16*

174

100 Ways to Love One Another (Continued)

82. **Comfort the fainthearted** *1 Thessalonians 5:14*

83. **Walk in the Spirit** *Galatians 5:16-23*

84. **Esteem God's ministers highly**
    1 Thessalonians 5:12-13

85. **Be hospitable to one another without grumbling**
    1 Peter 4:9

86. **Bless those who persecute you; bless and do not curse** *Romans 12:14*

87. **Love one another fervently with a pure heart**
    1 Peter 1:22

88. **Pray for others to prosper in all things and to be in health** *3 John 2*

89. **Do your share to cause growth of the body of Christ** *Ephesians 4:16*

90. **Bear with the scruples of the weak** *Romans 15:1*

91. **Do not covet** *Exodus 20:17*

92. **Do not bear false witness against your neighbor**
    Exodus 20:16

93. **Let love be without hypocrisy** *Romans 12:9*

100 Ways to Love One Another (Continued)

94. **Have compassion on the weary and scattered, like sheep having no shepherd** *Matthew 9:36*

95. **Be kindly affectionate to one another with brotherly love** *Romans 12:10*

96. **Pray for Christians to be strengthened with might through God's Spirit in the inner man** *Ephesians 3:16*

97. **Cover a multitude of sins** *1 peter 4:8*

98. **Teach others to build their house on Jesus' sayings (the Holy Bible), so their house will not fall** *Matthew 7:24-27*

99. **Be of the same mind toward one another** *Romans 12:14*

100. **Pursue what is good both for yourself and for all** *1 Thessalonians 5:15*

See: www.USAChristianMinistries.com for sharing tools

ᔕ *Prayer of Salvation...* ᔐ

God invites you to become a Christian. To become part of God's family, pray this prayer:

Father,

I confess with my mouth that Jesus Christ is Lord and I believe in my heart that You raised Jesus Christ from the dead. I call upon Jesus to forgive me for my sins. I ask for all the Holy Spirit has to give me so I can walk with You and serve You.

In Jesus' name. Amen.

ᔕᔐ

"...if you confess with your mouth the Lord Jesus and believe in your heart that God has raised Him from the dead, you will be saved. For with the heart one believes unto righteousness, and with the mouth confession is made unto salvation." Romans 10:9-10

Study Guide on next page

◈ *Group and Individual Study Guide* ◈

Chapter 1: The USA Needs God

1. Read Deuteronomy 30:15. What are God's best plans for our nation from the Holy Bible?
2. What are the points of our 1607 covenant?
3. How has God blessed you by living in the USA?

Chapter 2: The Settlers, Pilgrims, Washington, Adams... Made the USA a Christian Nation Forever

1. Read John 14:6. Why did our Founding Fathers say Christianity is superior to other religions?
2. Why do you believe Christianity is superior to other religions?
3. Why did our Founding Fathers make God's laws our laws?

Chapter 3: The Majority of the USA Are Christians

1. Read John 3:16. Do you believe that Jesus Christ is the Son of God who came to earth and died for our sins? Explain.
2. How significant is the Christian majority of the USA?
3. What are ways you can speak up for God and not be silent?

Chapter 4: The LORD is the God of the USA and We Are His People

1. Read Psalm 33:12. What are the two parts of the USA's Covenant with God™?
2. Explain the first part.
3. Explain the second part.

Chapter 5: Benefits of Our Christian Nation

1. What does Deuteronomy 28:1-2 and Leviticus 26:3-4 say causes God's blessings to come to a nation?
2. Where have you seen God's blessings in the USA?
3. Why does God want a Christian nation?

Chapter 6: What Causes Economic Decline and Loss of Freedoms

1. What does Galatians 6:7-8 mean? Also, what does Deut. 28:15 & Lev. 26:14-16 say causes curses to come to a nation?
2. What curses in Deut. 28 and Lev. 26 has the USA seen?
3. What are "root" sin issues and what are "fruit" curse issues?

Chapter 7: How to Answer God's Call for National Repentance

1. Read 2 Chronicles 7:14. What sins can you turn from? How?
2. Will you agree with God that the USA's sins need to end?
3. What can you do to help call the USA to national repentance?

Chapter 8: God's Mercy: Jesus' Sacrifice Forgives the USA

1. What does 1 John 1:7-9 mean for you personally?
2. How does the Holy Bible say sin is forgiven?

Chapter 9: God's Solution: Unite the USA in Christ

1. Read Ephesians 4:3. What does "endeavor to keep the unity of the Spirit" mean?
2. Why does God say unite the USA in Christ—and not unite the USA in Christians? What is the difference?

Chapter 10: Remove the Lie of "Separation of Church and State"

1. Read Philippians 2:11. Why is the Constitution a Christian document? What references to God does it have?
2. Why is "separation of church and state": 1) Not what our Founding Fathers practiced or intended; 2) Not Constitutional; 3) Not historical; and 4) Sin against God?

Chapter 11: God's Best Plans Are to Have No King But Jesus

1. Read Psalm 47:7-8. Explain what it means to live with Jesus as the USA's King.
2. Will you recognize Jesus as King of the USA? How?

179

Chapter 12: Twenty-one Ways to Pray for the USA
1. What does John 15:7 mean?
2. Do you use the Holy Bible to help you know how to pray?
3. What are common errors people make in prayer?

Chapter 13: Seek God First in Politics
1. Read Matthew 6:33. How does this verse apply to politics?
2. How can you and your church seek God first in politics?

Chapter 14: The Church Leads the USA
1. Read Matthew 28:18. Who has all power?
2. Who is salt and light? Who isn't salt and light?
3. How can you encourage Christians to lead our nation and build the USA on Jesus and the Holy Bible (Luke 6:47-49)?

Chapter 15: Action Plan: Your Assignment
1. Re-read Psalm 33:12. What does this mean?
2. Look at the suggestions given in this chapter. What can you do to make a difference for God in the USA?
3. Which Bible verses do you believe God wants you to share with people you know this week? Is there also an easy way you can share the Bible verses to reach a lot of people?

BONUS BOOKS
100 Ways to Love God
1. What does Mark 12:30 mean?
2. Why do you love God?
3. What are three ways that you could encourage someone else to love God?

100 Ways to Love One Another
1. Explain what Jesus means in John 13:34.
2. What are three ways that you can love one another as Jesus loved you?

Daily Live: The USA's Covenant With God™

It is a tangible thing for the USA to be right with God. He has told us how. Just follow this covenant:

Father,

As a Christian nation dedicated to You, we affirm our covenant:

- **You, the LORD, are the God of the USA and we are Your people. Jesus is our King. We obey what You say in the Holy Bible.**
- **We love You with all our heart, soul, mind and strength.**
- **We love one another as Jesus loved us.**
- **We ask You to forgive our sins by Jesus' sacrifice.**

In Jesus' name. Amen. *Psalm 33:12, Mark 12:30, John 13:34, 2 Chronicles 15:12, 1 John 1:7*

See www.USAChristianMinistries.com for tools.

Permission is given to reprint and pray The USA's Covenant with God™ in handouts, articles and on TV and radio provided the prayer is given for free and includes a reference to USAChristianMinistries.com. For other uses contact USA Christian Ministries to inquire about permission.

To Share: Please invite as many people as you can to join in praying and following this covenant prayer. There are covenant prayer cards and other items including a downloadable free print at: USAChristianMinistries.com. Also, think who you can give a copy of this book to.

For other books and items by Pastor Steven Andrew, or to help support USA Christian Ministries, see: USAChristianMinistries.com. May God bless you and the USA!

181